P9-DWO-335

CALGARY PUBLIC LIBRARY

SEP   2016

TABLE OF CONTENTS

CLEAN FOOD
– WHOLESOME FOOD THAT MAKES YOU FEEL GOOD

In this book, I write about the type of food I eat every day, food that makes me feel healthy and satisfied. Within these pages, you'll find lots of vegetables, fruits, and berries, as well as a small amount of protein; there are no dairy products and almost no gluten. Clean cooking is quite simple: it's a well-balanced diet that consists of tasty and clean food, which means it's processed as little as possible and contains few, if any, additives. It's easier to keep check on what you're feeding your body if you prepare your meals from scratch using wholesome, unadulterated ingredients. With this book, I hope to inspire you to enjoy great-tasting food that will also make you feel happy and healthy.

It's essential to listen to your body and understand what makes it feel good. In my case, while I am neither lactose- nor gluten-intolerant, I have found that I feel better and digest foods more easily whenever I abstain from dairy products and avoid gluten wherever possible. I'm happy to have found a diet that suits my lifestyle, and so I want to share my best recipes with you.

I first heard of the clean food trend a few years back, and it didn't take me long to embrace its principles whole-heartedly: no additives or anything else weird—just wholesome dishes prepared with clean, organic, and biodynamic ingredients.

I love raw food and nutritious juices, so those meals are integral to my daily diet. However, I also love sweets, and I'm not going to deprive myself of dessert once in a while. Here, I indulge in healthier options that are packed with energy and nutrition; for example, I'll use honey and dates instead of refined white sugar.

This is a collection of some of my best recipes for everyday meals, and I hope you will enjoy clean cooking and eating without gluten or dairy products, too. Eat well, and feel great!

Elisabeth Johansson

IN THE MOOD FOR GOOD FOOD!

CLEAN COOKING

Clean cooking is my own personal take on clean food, a concept that has taken hold in the United States, as well as the rest of the world. To eat "clean" means to consume pure, nutritious food, while avoiding processed, nutrition-deficient food products. It means choosing natural, organic food with few or no additives (this is entirely up to you, according to your level of commitment). In my personal life, I have found a way of living, cooking, and eating that's easy to follow; indeed, you can make simple choices for each meal without needlessly complicating things.

You won't find dairy products within the pages of *Clean Cooking*; however, you will encounter mustard, vinegar, and cellophane noodles. Opt for clean ingredients, fruits, vegetables, and sensible portions of meat, fish, and poultry. Deli meats are not included here, as all of them are processed and are thus too salty or too smoked.

"Raw rood" refers to ingredients that have not been heated beyond the temperature of 107.6°F–113°F (42°C–45°C). I love including raw food in my diet, either as one of the ingredients in a cooked dish or as an entire meal that is composed of only raw foods. I like preparing raw food desserts and raw food treats, where I can steer clear of refined white sugar. I usually carry a piece of fruit or some nuts in my bag when the occasional craving for sweets arises between meals, but another option is to mix your own snack pack, with nuts and dried berries like goji or mulberries, and carry it around with you. It's not a bad idea to include a small piece of dark chocolate, too.

We're all unique individuals, and so we react to food and health issues in a myriad of ways. It can take time to understand your own body's cues, and I have learned to listen to mine with a keen ear. Four years ago, I began to rethink my diet because my kidneys were kicking up a fuss and my stomach wasn't working like it should. I tried different tactics, one of which was to stop using dairy products little by little. I continued to eat cheese for a while, but after a few years I put an end to that as well.

I have also drastically reduced my intake of foods containing gluten, especially since cereals and products with gluten typically contain a lot of starch, which turns into sugar when digested by the body. What has allowed me to keep on eating bread is my homemade gluten-free rustic bread, the recipe for which you'll find on page 62. It is super tasty and very satisfying, making it perfect for starting the day. It's excellent for digestion; plus, it's easy to make! Sometimes, for breakfast, I'll drink freshly squeezed juice with a boost of something from the superfood list on page 15. Or, I'll tuck into some chia pudding, which I'll have prepared the night before. I also think that eggs and oatmeal are a great way to begin the day. I make the oatmeal by cooking flaxseed or other seeds, which I then top with sliced banana or blueberries, grated apple, cinnamon, and oat milk. For lunch and dinner, I'll have vegetables, root vegetables, meat, fish, poultry, and lentils—just like in the recipes of this book.

You gain so much when you find health through food and your stomach. Your disposition is sunnier when you feel good, you're able to manage more in your daily life, and you'll have more energy overall. Your immune system grows stronger, inflammations are stopped in their tracks, and your skin looks healthier and clearer.

Eating clean food has become a lifestyle that feels right for me, and it's really quite easy to follow. I also love the way clean food is prepared, where each ingredient has a chance to shine by showing off its particular flavor, color, and character on the plate. The food is simple and uncomplicated. I avoid all simple carbohydrates such as pasta, couscous, rice, potatoes, and cereal-based breads, and turn to quinoa, brown rice, buckwheat, oat groats, root vegetables, and lentils instead, which keep blood sugar more level.

I hope you'll feel inspired by this book and that it will help lead the way to your greatest health and well-being!

Live well—feel good! Good luck!

GLUTEN-FREE BAKING

FLOURS AND GRAINS

BUCKWHEAT

Buckwheat flour looks similar to wheat flour, but it comes from an herbaceous plant that is related to rhubarb and sorrel and is naturally gluten-free. Its seed is finely ground into flour.

Because buckwheat flour lacks gluten, the texture of baked goods made with it tends to be dense, more like sponge cake rather than sourdough bread.

Buckwheat works well in recipes for scones, muffins, and pancakes.

Buckwheat is a rich source of nutrients; it contains minerals, essential amino acids, potassium, magnesium, phosphorus, iron, and vitamin B. You can find buckwheat in the form of groats as well as crushed buckwheat and rolled buckwheat, where whole seeds are processed by sending them through heavy rollers.

CORN FLOUR

This particular flour is made from sweet corn, which is a member of the grass family. Corn flour is milled from dried whole corn kernels. The flour is light yellow, and it contains antioxidants, essential fatty acids, and minerals such as magnesium, iron, potassium, zinc, and vitamin B.

CORNSTARCH

Cornstarch is extracted from the corn kernel's endosperm. It's commonly used as a binder and texture enhancer and is a good option for thickening gluten-free sauces. Make sure to dissolve the cornstarch in some cold water before adding it to warm liquids, or else it can become lumpy.

Cornstarch is also known as maizena.

POTATO FLOUR

Potato starch is extracted from the liquid used to soak grated potatoes. The starch sinks to the bottom of the container, after which it is collected and dried. Potato flour—or starch—can be used in the same way as cornstarch.

ROLLED OATS

Oat flour is naturally gluten-free, but it's best to be careful with it since oats are often processed in the same machines and manufacturing plants as other flours. Double-check that the label on the package states "pure oats."

Rolled oats are made from oat groats that are steamed and then crushed between heavy rollers into flakes.

Oats contain large amounts of thiamine, iron, fibers, and antioxidants.

FIBER FLOURS

POTATO FLAKES

Potato flakes are a type of starch that is extracted from potatoes. The starch is dried and processed with heavy rollers to produce flakes. These flakes absorb a lot of liquid by binding to it, which keeps bread moist.

They are also rich in fiber, which helps to slow down digestion. This in turn keeps blood glucose levels lower and more stable.

PSYLLIUM SEED FLOUR

This flour is made from ground psyllium husks. The seeds contain a gel-like substance that increases in volume and binds to moisture. This type of flour makes the dough more workable and pliable, which produces a more moist and less crumbly bread. Ground psyllium husk works well in breads, coffee cakes, and cookies.

"Fiber husk" and "psyllium" are two product names for psyllium seed flour.

NUT AND ALMOND FLOURS

ALMOND FLOUR

Almond flour is made from finely ground sweet almonds. It's a rich source of omega-6 fatty acids (which could bring on an inflammatory response in those who have a sensitivity to it), and it oxidizes when heated. This is why almond flour is best suited for no-bake goods, such as raw food balls and bars.

HAZELNUT (FILBERT) FLOUR

Hazelnut flour is made from finely ground hazelnuts. It works particularly well in granola, cookies, and pie dough. Hazelnut flour has a nutty taste and is very rich in fiber.

COCONUT FLOUR

Coconut flour is made from dried and ground coconut flesh. It is extremely rich in fiber and absorbs a lot of moisture. Coconut flour is great to use in cookies and pancakes.

ALTERNATIVES TO WHITE SUGAR

You don't need to depend on refined white sugar as a sweetening agent. Several alternatives exist, many of which contain important enzymes and trace elements. Here are a few choice options, all of which impart a natural sweetness and tasty end results.

AGAVE

Agave syrup is made from the agave plant, which is native to South America. The syrup is extremely sweet and its fructose content is very high (as is its GI index rating), which means it should be used sparingly. Use half the amount as you would honey.

DATES

The most commonly available type of date in grocery stores today is the Medjool. They are soft, sweet, and extremely rich in fiber. Originally from the Middle East, they are now cultivated in California. The fruit grows from the very top of the date palm. Dates not only add sweetness but also impart a nice texture to coffee cakes, cookie balls, and smoothies. Their taste is reminiscent of dark syrup, caramel and vanilla.

HONEY

There are a wide variety of honeys to choose from. Raw honey is in its most natural state when it has not been heated, which allows it to retain more of its natural enzymes and trace elements. It is common practice, however, to heat honey in order to prevent crystallization. If you're lucky, you can find the cleanest and finest virgin honey that is drip-extracted from beeswax cakes instead of honey that is obtained via centrifugal extraction.

Honey can be used in both baking and cooking applications. It's sweeter than white sugar, so you'll need to use less of it.

COCONUT SUGAR

Coconut sugar is extracted from the sap of several types of coconut palms that are mainly found in Asia. Almost one gallon (3.8 liters) of sap is needed to produce just over 1 pound (500 grams) of palm sugar. This sugar has a low GI index rating and contains large amounts of minerals, potassium, magnesium, phosphorus, zinc, iron, several different B vitamins, and several amino acids.

The sap is heated during the extraction process, which gives the sugar a nice caramel flavor reminiscent of molasses or muscovado sugar. Coconut sugar can be substituted wherever white sugar is used.

MAPLE SYRUP

Maple syrup is made from the sap that has been extracted from the sugar maple tree. The sap is boiled to evaporate its water content. It takes 15 gallons (60 liters) of sap to produce 1 quart (1 liter) of syrup, which is why this gleaming, golden syrup can be so expensive. Cheaper versions are often diluted with white sugar, so it's important to read the ingredients label carefully.

Maple syrup is a wonderful topping for ice cream and pancakes, as well as a great sweetener for drinks.

SUPERFOODS

Superfoods are foods with a high concentration of nutrition. They can be found in powder, seed, or grain form. Don't forget that everyday fresh berries are also bursting with wholesome nutrition.

ACAI POWDER

Acai powder comes from the acai palm, also called cabbage palm. Its berries taste like a blend of berries and chocolate, and they contain high levels of antioxidants; vitamins E, C, B1, B2, and B3; calcium; phosphorus; potassium; protein; amino acids; and fatty acids.

CAROB

Carob is milled from the dried legume, or pod, of the St.-John's-bread tree. This light brown powder is rich in nutrients, such as vitamins B1, B2, and B6; potassium; calcium; copper; magnesium; iron; manganese; and nickel.

Carob powder has a light, sweet taste, blending the flavors of toffee and milk chocolate. It's often incorporated into smoothies, granola, bars, cookie balls, cookies, ice cream, and hot chocolate.

CHIA SEEDS

Chia seeds come from a flowering Salvia plant native to Mexico. They contain high levels of α-linolenic acid, omega-3 fatty acids, protein, and amino acids. To derive the most from these nutrients, grind the seeds in a spice grinder before eating them. Chia seeds contain large amounts of fiber, which helps keep blood sugar levels in check. The seeds can be incorporated into custards and oatmeal, as well as used in baking and in drinks.

GOJI BERRIES

The goji berry, one of the world's most nutritious fruits, comes from the Chinese boxthorn plant. It contains extremely high levels of vitamins A, B1, B2, B3, and C; antioxidants; beta carotene; amino acids; minerals; phosphorus; iron; calcium; copper; manganese; selenium; and many wholesome trace elements.

Its flavor will call to mind dried raspberries, rosehip, and cranberry with its pleasant, tangy, tartness. Substitute goji berries for raisins as they go well with granola, muesli, fruit bars, or balls. Sprinkle them over oatmeal, or a fruit or vegetable salad.

HEMP SEEDS

Hemp seeds, also called hemp hearts when hulled, come from the hemp plant. They are small, soft, and contain plenty of amino acids, essential fatty acids, and protein. They can be used in place of sesame seeds.

Hemp seeds can be used in, or as a covering for, balls, bars, cookies. You can also add them to smoothies or sprinkle them over oatmeal, vegetables, and salads.

CACAO NIBS

Cacao nibs are roasted cacao beans that have been broken into small pieces. Cacao contains large quantities of antioxidants that are easily absorbed by the body. Cacao is also rich in magnesium and zinc.

MACA

The maca plant, a relative of the radish, grows in Peru and around the Andes mountain range. It contains vitamins B1, B2, B12, C, and E, as well as minerals, fatty acids, and several micronutrients.

Do use caution, however, when using maca if you suffer from heart or cardiovascular problems.

MULBERRIES

These are small, light-brown fruit featuring a happy combination of vitamin C and iron. They are often used in dried form. Mulberries have a sweet, nutty taste that is very flavorful, especially when added to granola, for example.

SPIRULINA POWDER

This green powder is made from the spirulina algae. It is rich in chlorophyll, vitamins, minerals, and essential fatty acids.

Spirulina powder has a special flavor that combines well with fresh citrus and ginger. The powder is typically added to smoothies, juices, nutritional shots, breads, and granola.

WHEATGRASS POWDER

Wheatgrass powder is packed with chlorophyll, vitamins, some minerals, and essential fatty acids.

This powder can be added to smoothies, juices, and nutritional shots. To make fresh wheatgrass juice, pass natural wheatgrass through a juicer, perhaps along with a few tart green apples.

ALTERNATIVES TO DAIRY PRODUCTS

Milk is the collective term used for dairy-free "dairy drinks." It's easy to concoct your own favorite milk and add in flavors according to season and/or personal taste. All the recipes below make about 1 quart (1 liter).

GREEN MILK

1¼ cups (300 ml) almond milk
2 cups + 3 tbsp (500 ml) spinach
2–3 leaves of kale
2 dates
Ice cubes

Blend almond milk with the spinach, kale, dates, and ice. Strain through a nut milk bag or a piece of cheesecloth, and wring its contents to extract the milk. Serve immediately.

TIP! If you prefer creamier milk, mix in some banana, avocado, or Galia melon. The fatty acids in the almonds facilitate the body's absorption of some of the vitamins in the vegetables.

ALMOND MILK

1¼ cups (300 ml) skinless almonds
3¾ cups (900 ml) water
½ tsp (2 ml) liquid honey

Soak the almonds in water for about 8 hours. Drain the almonds, saving the water. Rinse the almonds. Blend the almonds with half of the reserved water, and then add in the rest of the water.
   Strain through a nut milk bag or piece of cheesecloth, and wring it to extract the milk.
   Keep the milk refrigerated; it will keep for about 3 days.

CHOCOLATE MILK

2 tbsp cacao
4⅓ cups (1000 ml) almond milk
2 tsp honey
1 tsp ground cardamom
1 tsp ground cinnamon

Blend all ingredients with an immersion blender. Serve the drink warm or cold.
   Keep the milk refrigerated; it will keep for 1 to 2 days.

COCONUT MILK

1⅓ cups (400 ml) grated
   coconut
3⅓ cups (800 ml) water
⅘ cup (200 ml) coconut water
¼ vanilla bean or ¼ tsp (1 krm)
   vanilla seeds

Blend coconut, water, and
coconut water. Split the vanilla
bean lengthwise and place it
into the milk.

   Drain through a nut milk bag
or piece of cheesecloth, and
wring it to extract the milk.

   Keep the milk refrigerated;
it will keep for 2 to 3 days.

HAZELNUT (FILBERT) MILK

1¼ cups (300 ml) peeled
   hazelnuts (filberts)
2 dates, pitted or 1 tsp palm
   sugar
3¾ cups (900 ml) water

Soak the hazelnuts for 8 hours.
Drain the water—saving the
water—and rinse the nuts.
Blend the nuts and dates with
half the amount of reserved
water, and then add in the
rest of the water. Strain the
milk through a nut milk bag
or piece of cheesecloth, and
wring it to extract the milk.

   Keep the milk refrigerated;
it will keep for 2 to 3 days.

Tip! This drink is very tasty
when flavored with cacao,
cardamom, or cinnamon.
Enjoy it warm or cold.

CASHEW MILK

*Follow the recipe for hazelnut
milk, but substitute 1¼ cup
cashew nuts for the hazelnuts.*

OAT MILK

1¼ cups (300 ml) rolled oats
4⅓ cups (1000 ml) water
2 tbsp unflavored oil (e.g.,
   cold-pressed canola)
Pinch of salt

Grind the oats in a food
processor. Add water, oil, and
salt. Blend together for a few
seconds, and then let stand for
5 to 10 minutes.

   Strain through a nut milk
bag or piece of cheesecloth,
and wring it to extract the
milk.

   Keep the milk refrigerated;
it will keep for 2 to 3 days.

CLEAN COOKING

MILKSHAKES

Makes a delicious breakfast, snack, or dessert. Both recipes yield two glasses of wonderful beverage.

STRAWBERRY MILKSHAKE

2 bananas
1⅔ cups (400 ml) strawberries
1⅓–2 cups + 3 tbsp (400–500 ml) milk of your choice (e.g., oat, almond, or rice)
¼ tsp (1 krm) vanilla powder

EXTRA BOOST
3–4 tbsp hemp hearts

Peel and slice the bananas. Clean and slice the strawberries. Store the bananas and strawberries in the freezer until frozen.

Blend the bananas and strawberries, and add in milk and vanilla powder. For an extra heart-healthy boost, mix in the hemp hearts.

CHOCOLATE CHIP MILKSHAKE

2 bananas, frozen
2 dates, pitted
1¾ oz (50 g) dark chocolate, chopped
1⅓–2 cups + 3 tbsp (4–500 ml) milk of your choice—oat, almond or rice
4 tbsp vegan chocolate sauce, see recipe on page 131

EXTRA BOOST
1 tbsp cacao nibs

Peel and slice the bananas, then place them in the freezer until frozen.

Process the bananas in a blender. Add dates, chocolate, and milk. For an extra magnesium boost, sprinkle in some cacao nibs.

To serve, drizzle lukewarm chocolate sauce at the bottom of the glasses. Pour in the milk and use a straw to drink it up.

HEALTHY OPTIONS !

VEGAN "DAIRY"

PINE NUT "CREAM CHEESE"
Serves 4

1¼ cups (300 ml) pine nuts
3½ tbsp (50 ml) olive oil
2 tbsp water
2 tbsp lemon juice, freshly squeezed
¼ tsp salt

Process the nuts in a food processor, adding the olive oil and the water drop by drop. Add in the lemon juice and salt. Mix until smooth.

TIP! Perfect for salads and vegetarian dishes.

CASHEW MAYONNAISE
Serves 4

1 cup + 1½ tbsp (250 ml) natural cashew nuts
3½ tbsp (50 ml) olive oil
2 tbsp water
2–3 tbsp lemon juice, freshly squeezed
¼ tsp salt

Process the nuts in a food processor. Add in olive oil, water, lemon juice, and salt. Mix until smooth.

TIP! This makes a handy base for a dip, as well as a side for meat, fish, or vegan dishes.

EASY TO MAKE!

VEGAN / RAW FOOD VANILLA CRÈME
Serves 4 to 6

2½ cups (300 g/600 ml)
   cashew nuts
7 oz (half a can/200 g)
   coconut cream
½ vanilla bean
⅖ cup (100 ml) maple syrup

Soak the cashew nuts in cold water for one hour.

Split the vanilla bean lengthwise.

Drain the nuts and blend them with the coconut cream. Add the seeds from the vanilla bean and the maple syrup, and mix again.

TIP! A vanilla "crème" made with cashew nuts and coconut cream makes a great accompaniment to fruit (chunks of cinnamon-dusted apple, for example, or fresh berries).

Use the second half of the vanilla bean to make your own vanilla sugar. Let the vanilla bean dry at room temperature for 48 hours. Mix the bean with 3 tbsp of coconut sugar. Sift the vanilla sugar into an airtight container.

NUT BUTTERS

Delicious with pancakes, oatmeal, chia seed pudding, and fresh fruit, like slices of apple. Nuts release their oil when they are heated or lightly roasted, which facilitates the mixing.

PEANUT BUTTER
makes about 1 cup (250 ml)

1¼ cups (300 ml) natural, raw peanuts
¼ (1 krm) sea salt

Grind the nuts until they form a smooth paste.

PISTACHIO BUTTER
makes about 1 cup (250 ml)

1¼ cups (300 ml) raw pistachio nuts, shelled

Mix the nuts until they form a smooth paste.

TIP! Add 2 tbsp honey for a sweeter butter.

CASHEW BUTTER
makes about 1 cup (250 ml)

1¼ cups (300 ml) cashew nuts

Grind the nuts until they form a smooth paste.

ALMOND BUTTER
makes about 1 cup (250 ml)

1¼ cups (300 ml) sweet, raw almonds

Blanch and skin the almonds. Grind the almonds until they form a smooth paste.

HAZELNUTELLA
makes about 1¼ to 1⅔ cups (300–400 ml)

¾ cup + 3 tbsp (200 ml) hazelnuts (filberts)
3½ oz (100 g) dark chocolate; 56–64% cacao
½ cup (100 ml) coconut cream
¼ cup (50 ml) coconut sugar
¼ tsp (1 krm) salt
1 cup + 1½ tbsp (250 ml) cacao powder
3½ tbsp (50 ml) coconut oil

Roast hazelnuts in a dry skillet. Rub off the skins with a clean dishtowel. Grind the nuts with the chocolate.

Bring the coconut cream, coconut sugar, salt, and cacao powder to a boil in a saucepan. Let the mixture cool to 131–140°F (55–60°C). Add to the nuts and mix. Add the coconut oil a little at a time while the mixer is on.

RAINBOW JUICES

Colorful fruits and vegetables contain lots of different nutrients and antioxidants, so it's important to eat some of every color. For instance, carotene can be found in orange-colored root vegetables, such as carrots, and in fruits, such as apricots. Carotene is converted to vitamin A in the liver and is beneficial for the eyes. Green leafy vegetables contain chlorophyll, which gives us vitamin K, which in turn helps build our skeleton; chlorophyll is also good for maintaining healthy skin and is packed with antioxidants. Below, you'll find flavor combinations that I find incredibly tasty.

Make juice from a choice of different colors or mix several in each glass. Simply match and combine what you have at home or go with what your taste buds tell you!

If you'd like to boost your metabolic rate, spice up your juice by adding some chili pepper, ginger, or cayenne pepper.

YELLOW
Pineapple
Orange
Lemon
Grapefruit
Coconut water

EXTRA BOOST
Ginger
Fresh turmeric
Mint

ORANGE
Orange
Cantaloupe
Grapefruit
Mandarin orange
Carrot

EXTRA BOOST
Freshly grated ginger
Fresh turmeric
Sea buckthorn juice
Maca powder

RED
Blood orange
Ruby red grapefruit
Raspberries
Strawberries
Watermelon

EXTRA BOOST
Acai powder
Freshly grated ginger
Maca powder

DRINK THE RAINBOW!

GREEN
Celery
Galia melon or Honeydew
   melon
Green apples
Kale
Cucumber
Spinach

EXTRA BOOST
Mint
Spirulina
Wheatgrass, fresh
   or powder

DEEP RED
Blood orange
Ruby Red grapefruit
Red apples
Beets
Red cabbage
Cranberry juice

EXTRA BOOST
Acai powder
Freshly grated ginger

BLUE
Blueberries
Blackberries
Black currants
Watermelon or
   Honeydew melon
Grapes, black or red

EXTRA BOOST
Acai powder
Carob (seed flour from
   the St.-John's-bread
   tree)
Fresh grated ginger

KVASS

Kvass is a lightly fermented beverage that hails from Russia. Originally, it was made from a mix of malt, rye flour, and water that was left to ferment until slightly carbonated; its taste calls to mind the Swedish non-alcoholic drink called svagdricka. Kvass contains enzymes and bacteria that are beneficial for stomach health and for digestion. While the following recipes feature some fresh twists on the drink by being flavored with fruit, berries, honey, and ginger, they all still build on the original method of fermenting beverages in order to get a lightly sparkling, flavored water. This is a real favorite to cool down with on sultry summer days.

The recipes yield approximately ½ gallon (2 liters), ready to serve.

KVASS WITH LEMON, PEACH, AND STRAWBERRIES

4 peaches
1⅔ cups (400 ml) fresh
     strawberries
2 lemons
2 tbsp liquid honey
1 tsp ginger, freshly grated
½ gallon (2 liters) pure tap
     water, filtered water, or non-
     carbonated mineral water

Slice the peaches, strawberries, and lemons. Place them in one large jar or two smaller glass jars. Add in honey, ginger, and water. It's important to keep a good 1-inch (3 cm) gap between the jar's lid and its contents, since pressure will build within the jar. Stir thoroughly to make sure everything is mixed.

Let the jar sit for 2 to 3 days at room temperature. Shake it a few times each day to make sure that everything stays well mixed and that no bacteria form on the liquid's surface. Time can vary for kvass to ripen: in a colder room it could take up to 6 or 7 days. Taste the kvass—it's ready when the flavor is fresh and sweet, and the water is sparkling. Strain the kvass and pour it over ice.

KVASS WITH PLUMS, BLACKBERRIES, AND RASPBERRIES

4 lilac plums
1¼ cups (300 ml) fresh
     raspberries
1¼ cups (300 ml) fresh
     blackberries
2 tbsp liquid honey
1 tsp ginger, freshly grated
½ gallon (2 liters) pure tap
     water, filtered water, or non-
     carbonated mineral water

Remove the pit from the plums, and cut the plums into chunks. Put the plums and berries in a large glass jar or in two smaller glass jars. Add in honey, ginger, and water. It's important to keep a good 1-inch (3 cm) gap between the jar's lid and its contents, since pressure will build within the jar. Stir thoroughly to make sure everything is mixed.

Let the jar sit for 2 to 3 days at room temperature. Shake it a few times each day to make sure everything stays well mixed and that no bacteria form on the liquid's surface. Time can vary for kvass to ripen: in a colder room it could take up to 6 or 7 days. Taste the kvass—it's ready when the flavor is fresh and sweet, and the water is sparkling. Strain the kvass and pour it over ice.

KVASS WITH ORANGE AND PINEAPPLE

2 oranges
1 pineapple
2 tbsp liquid honey
1 tsp ginger, freshly grated or
     fresh turmeric
½ gallon (2 liters) pure tap
     water, filtered water, or non-
     carbonated mineral water

Peel the oranges and cut them into chunks. Remove the green leaves (crown) from the pineapple and rinse the whole fruit. Cut the fruit into chunks, leaving the peel intact. Put the fruit in a large glass jar or in two smaller glass jars.

Add in honey, ginger, and water. It's important to keep a good one-inch (3 cm) gap between the jar's lid and its contents, since pressure will build within the jar. Stir thoroughly to make sure everything is mixed.

Let the jar sit for 2 to 3 days at room temperature. Shake it a few times each day to make sure everything stays well mixed and that no bacteria form on the liquid's surface. Time can vary for kvass to ripen: in a colder room it could take up to 6 or 7 days. Taste the kvass—it's ready when the flavor is fresh and sweet, and the water is sparkling. Strain the kvass and pour it over ice.

TIP! The kvass will keep in the refrigerator for about a week, but it is critical to store it in sterilized containers to avoid having mold grow on the kvass. Leave washed jars in the oven for 20 minutes at a temperature of 212°F (100°C). Pour the kvass into the jars once they've cooled. Leave the lid on slightly loose, preferably putting a piece of cloth, fastened with a rubber band, around the opening to protect the jar's contents. Or, release the pressure building up in the jars by opening them once a day.

KEY LIME JUICE

This is a healthy and refreshing blend of coconut water, honey, and lime. A few years ago, coconut water became extremely trendy in Hollywood—various celebrities were spotted quenching their thirst with it following their workout sessions—and the trend quickly spread across the world. Coconut water has been called nature's own sports drink as it contains large amounts of potassium, calcium, zinc, and vitamins B and C. Key lime juice, when combined with nuts, makes an excellent snack.

1 quart (1 liter) coconut water
4 limes
1–2 tbsp liquid honey

Pour the coconut water into a pitcher or glass jar. Cut two of the limes in half, and squeeze their juice into the jug or the glass jar. Wash and slice the other two limes, and add them to the water. Add honey to taste, and pour over ice.

Serves 4

KOMBUCHA "SANGRIA"

This is an alcohol-free version of sangria made with wholesome kombucha, a raw food beverage made from fermented tea. Kombucha originally hails from China, where it is called the elixir of life. It provides, among other things, useful enzymes, vitamin B, and minerals.

1 quart (1 liter) kombucha (with raspberries and lemon, for example)
1 orange
1 lemon
⅘ cup (200 ml) strawberries
Ice

Pour the kombucha into a pitcher or glass jar. Wash and slice the orange and lemon, and add the slices to the kombucha. Rinse and cut the strawberries in half, and add them to the mixture. Add ice and serve immediately.

29

WATERMELON DRINK

This is a sweet and refreshing drink that is ideal for serving a crowd.

1 watermelon
4 limes
1⅔ cups (400 ml) carbonated
    mineral water
Ice
Mint for garnish, optional

Remove the rind from three-fourths of the watermelon, and cut the flesh into chunks. Process the chunks in a juice extractor.

Pour the juice into a pitcher or glass jar.

Juice the limes, and add the lime juice to the watermelon juice. Wash and slice the remaining two limes and add them to the juice. Cut the rest of the melon into chunks and add them in, too.

Pour in the mineral water and add some mint. Pour over ice.

ORANGE ZINGER

A real jolt of vitamins, loaded with carotene.

DRINK
2 oranges, yellow or lightly
   tinted blood oranges
1 lemon
2 carrots
¼–¾-inch (1–2 cm) ginger,
   freshly grated
Ice

EXTRA BOOST
AND FLAVORING
A fresh piece of turmeric
¼ tsp (1 krm) cayenne pepper

Peel the oranges and the lemon. Cut the fruit into chunks. Wash and peel the carrots, and cut them up. Process all the drink ingredients in a juice extractor.

If you wish to boost nutrients with a piece of fresh turmeric, add it along with the fruit into the juicer. Finally, stir in the cayenne pepper. Pour over lots of ice.

JUICES AND SMOOTHIES

31

Serves 2

KALE SMOOTHIE

The nutritious kale brims with iron. To facilitate the body's uptake of iron, you should add some vitamin C to the kale.

SMOOTHIE
1 lb (500 g) (generous) kale
1 orange
2 bananas
½ fresh pineapple
Fresh mint for garnish

EXTRA BOOST
1 tsp spirulina powder or
   wheatgrass powder

Rinse and check the kale for stray grit, and chop it into pieces. Process the kale in a juice extractor. Peel the orange and put it through the juicer.

Peel the bananas and the pineapple, and cut them into chunks. Blend the banana and pineapple, and mix them with the kale and pineapple juice. By all means, boost it by adding in some spirulina or wheatgrass powder. Garnish with fresh mint leaves.

TIP! Store the banana and pineapple chunks in the freezer for several hours to make the smoothie extra cold and tasty. You can also add in some crushed ice. You'll find the recipe for the balls in the picture on page 146.

Serves 2

HELLO SUN! SMOOTHIE

A vibrant yellow burst of vitamin C, covered in nutritious seeds!

SMOOTHIE
2 oranges
2 carrots
1 mango
1 banana

EXTRA BOOST
¼-inch ginger, peeled and
    finely grated
A knob of fresh turmeric root,
    peeled and finely grated

TOPPING
Pumpkin seeds
Sunflower seeds
Buckwheat flakes

Peel the oranges and process them in a juice extractor, or leave the peel on and juice them with a manual press.

Peel the carrots, cut them in chunks, and process them in the extractor. Mix the orange and carrot juices together.

Peel the mango and banana, and cut them into chunks. Blend them, and then mix them with the orange and carrot juice.

TIP! Leave the mango and banana chunks in the freezer for several hours. This will make the smoothie frosty and delicious.

ENERGY SHOTS

Start your day with a shot of concentrated energy. Or, take a reviving shot in the afternoon instead of the usual cup of coffee. Today, there are many quality juice extractors on the market, and at reasonable prices, too! Each recipe here makes enough for approximately 2 shot glasses of wholesome juice.

GREEN CHLOROPHYLL

1 container of wheatgrass
1 lemon
1 lime
1 green apple
¼-inch fresh ginger, peeled

Snip the wheatgrass with scissors. Peel the lemon and lime and cut them into chunks.

Cut the apple into chunks. Layer all the ingredients and process them in a juice extractor. Pour the juice into shot glasses, and bottoms up!

ORANGE, CAROTENE, AND VITAMIN C

1 carrot
1 orange
1 whole turmeric root
¼-inch fresh ginger, peeled

Wash or peel the carrot and cut it into chunks. Peel the orange and cut it into chunks. Process all ingredients in the juicer. Pour into shot glasses, and bottoms up!

RED BOOST OF IRON, THE RED MEDICINE

1 beet
1¾ oz (50 g) of spinach
1 leaf of kale
⅖ cup (100 ml) cranberry juice or pomegranate juice
1 tsp acai powder

Peel and rinse the beet thoroughly to remove every speck of soil. Cut the beet into pieces, layer with spinach and kale, and process in the juicer.

Mix the juice with cranberry or pomegranate juice and acai powder. Pour into shot glasses, and bottoms up!

IT'S HEALTHY

Serves 2

BLACK CURRANT SMOOTHIE

This is a tart and full-bodied smoothie bursting with vitamin C and antioxidants. If you prefer, you can substitute almond milk for oat milk.

1⅔ cups (400 ml) frozen black currants
⅖ cup (100 ml) frozen blueberries
2 bananas
2 tbsp liquid honey
1⅔ cups (400 ml) of oat milk
3 tbsp dark chocolate, chopped
4 bunches of fresh black or red currants

Blend the black currants and blueberries. Peel the bananas, cut them into chunks, and add them and the honey to the mix. Pour in the oat milk and blend quickly for a smoothie without lumps.

Add 2 tbsp chopped chocolate and blend again. Pour the smoothie into glasses, and top them with the rest of the chopped chocolate and fresh currants.

Serves 2

BLUEBERRY AND COCONUT SMOOTHIE

This is my all-time favorite smoothie! In early spring when I do my annual detox, I always begin with this smoothie as it tastes wonderful and fills me up completely. It's a true kick-start to summer! Frozen blueberries turn this into a malt-like beverage, but if you're not looking for texture that's quite as rich and cold, defrost the berries first. Personally, I love the frozen version, which is very frosty and viscous.

SMOOTHIE
2 bananas
2 cups (500 ml) (heaping) frozen blueberries
1 can of coconut milk, 14 fl oz (400 g)
⅖ cup (100 ml) fresh blueberries
Dried coconut chips

EXTRA BOOST
2 tsp acai powder

Peel the bananas and cut them into chunks. First blend the blueberries, and then add the bananas. Blend again and add in the coconut milk. Blend until smooth, without any lumps.

Pour into glasses or glass jars. Top with fresh blueberries and coconut chips.

TIP! You'll find coconut chips in well-stocked health food stores and grocery stores.

GREEN POWER !

Serves 2

GREEN MACHINE

A real boost of chlorophyll! If you like celery, juice a stalk of it along with the rest of the ingredients. If you don't like it, you can use mint instead. It can be part of the juice or its garnish.

3½ oz (100 g) spinach
2 green apples
½ Galia melon
½ cucumber
1 lime
2 celery stalks, for garnish
Ice

Rinse and check the spinach thoroughly for any grit. Cut the apples into quarters. Peel the melon and remove the seeds. Then, cut the melon and cucumber into chunks. Peel the lime with a sharp knife, and cut the lime into chunks. Process all the ingredients in the juice extractor.

Place ice in glasses and pour in the juice. Cut the celery stalks in half lengthwise and garnish the juice with the celery stalks and leaves.

CHIA SEED PUDDING

Chia seed pudding can be eaten both as a breakfast and a snack. It is filling and it helps keep blood sugar on a healthy, even keel. All the recipes make 1 to 2 servings.

VANILLA CHIA PUDDING

1¼ cups (200 ml) almond, rice, or oat milk
¼ cup (scant) (50 ml) chia seeds
¼ tsp (1 krm) vanilla powder

Mix all ingredients thoroughly to avoid lumps, and divide the pudding between individual bowls or jars. Refrigerate overnight.

A serving example: serve with raspberries, blueberries, chunks of avocado, and a drizzle of honey. Or, you could have it with slices of apple and ground cinnamon or cardamom.

BLUEBERRY CHIA PUDDING

¼ cup (50 ml) blueberries
⅔ cup (150 ml) almond, rice or oat milk
1 tbsp liquid honey
⅓ cup (75 ml) chia seeds

TO SERVE
⅖ cup (100 ml) (generous) berries (e.g., raspberries and blueberries)
A drizzle of honey

Blend blueberries, the milk of your choice, and honey. Stir in the chia seeds thoroughly to avoid lumps, and divide the pudding between individual bowls or jars. Refrigerate overnight.

Top with raspberries and blueberries, and drizzle on some extra honey.

CHIA PUDDING WITH BANANA AND PEANUT BUTTER

½ banana
1 tsp peanut butter
½ tsp liquid honey
1¼ cups (200 ml) almond, rice, or oat milk
¼ tsp (1 krm) vanilla powder
⅓ cup (75 ml) chia seeds

TO SERVE
Ground cinnamon
Banana
Apple pieces
Honey, optional

Blend banana, peanut butter, honey, your choice of milk, and vanilla. Stir in the chia seeds thoroughly to avoid lumps, and divide the pudding between individual bowls or jars. Refrigerate overnight.

Top with cinnamon, banana, pieces of apple, and perhaps some extra honey.

RASPBERRY CHIA PUDDING

¼ cup (50 ml) raspberries
⅔ cup (150 ml) almond, rice or oat milk
½ tbsp liquid honey
¼ tsp (1 krm) vanilla powder
½ banana, peeled
⅓ cup (75 ml) chia seeds

TO SERVE
⅖ cup (100 ml) (generous) berries (e.g., raspberries and blueberries)
A drizzle of honey

Blend raspberries, your choice of milk, honey, vanilla, and banana. Stir in the chia seeds thoroughly to avoid lumps, and divide the pudding between individual bowls or jars. Refrigerate overnight.

Top with raspberries and blueberries, and drizzle with some extra honey.

Makes approximately 6 pancakes

BUCKWHEAT PANCAKES WITH BLUEBERRIES AND PEANUT BUTTER

These buckwheat pancakes are not only gluten- and dairy-free, they're also very easy to prepare. Buckwheat imparts a full-bodied taste. Maple syrup and non-dairy ice cream make great accompaniments, as do cinnamon-dusted apple slices sautéed in honey.

BUCKWHEAT PANCAKES
⅝ cup (75 g) buckwheat flour
1¼ cups (300 g) almond milk
2 large eggs
½ tsp vanilla powder
¼ tsp (1 krm) salt
Oil (neutral-tasting) for frying

RAW BLUEBERRY COMPOTE WITH HONEY
1¼ cups (300 ml) frozen
   blueberries, defrosted
2 tbsp liquid honey

SIDES
⅖ cup (100 ml) peanut butter
   (see recipe on page 22)
1¼ cups (300 ml) fresh
   strawberries

GARNISH
Fresh mint

Start by mashing the blueberries, and then mix them with the honey.

Whisk the buckwheat flour for the pancakes with half of the almond milk. Whisk until the batter is smooth. Add the eggs and the rest of the almond milk. Add vanilla and salt. Fry the pancakes on both sides in a little bit of oil until they are nicely browned.

Serve the pancakes with raw blueberry compote, strawberries, and peanut butter. Garnish with fresh mint.

Serves 4 to 6

BLUEBERRY OATMEAL

An excellent way to start to the day! Slice a banana onto the blueberry oatmeal and dust with powdered cinnamon for fantastic added flavor.

BLUEBERRY OATMEAL
1⅔ cups (400 ml) rolled oats
3¾ cups (900 ml) water
½ tsp salt
¼ cup (50 ml) (heaping)
    flaxseed
⅘ cup (200 ml) frozen
    blueberries

TO SERVE
⅘ cup (200 ml) fresh
    blueberries
1 tsp ground cinnamon
1 tbsp sunflower seeds
½ tbsp flaxseed
Oat or almond milk

Bring rolled oats, water, salt, and flaxseed to a boil. Stir and let simmer for a few minutes. Add in the frozen blueberries before bringing the oats to a boil again.

Serve the oatmeal with fresh blueberries, ground cinnamon, sunflower seeds, flaxseeds, and oat milk.

AMAZEBOWLS

Amazebowls have milk and peanut or almond butter as a base, and they make a great breakfast or snack. If you add in some acai, you'll have an acai bowl! Each bowl recipe makes 2 servings, and the granola recipe will make about 2½ cups (600 ml).

VERY BERRY ACAI BOWL

1 cup (250 ml) (generous) frozen berries (e.g., raspberries, strawberries, and blueberries)
½ banana
1 cup (250 ml) (generous) almond milk
2 tsp acai powder
½–1 tbsp peanut or almond butter

Blend all ingredients in a food processor or blender.

CHOCO COCO ACAI BOWL

2 bananas, sliced and frozen
1 cup (250 ml) (generous) coconut milk
1–2 tbsp raw cacao powder or cocoa powder
2 tsp acai powder
½–1 tbsp peanut or almond butter

Blend all ingredients in a food processor or blender.

TIP! All bowls can be served with berries, sliced banana, chunks of avocado, coconut chips, and chopped chocolate, for example, and drizzled with honey.

GREEN PASSION AMAZEBOWL

½ fresh pineapple
1¾ oz (50 g) spinach
2 leaves of kale
1 mango, peeled, cut into ⅓ x ⅓-inch pieces, frozen
1 avocado
⅘ cup (200 ml) coconut milk
½–1 tbsp peanut or almond butter

Peel and cut the pineapple into chunks. Tear the kale into small pieces. Layer pineapple, kale, and spinach, and process them in a juice extractor.

Blend the mango and avocado. Add in the vegetable juice, coconut milk, and nut butter.

ACAI GRANOLA

⅘ cup (200 ml) rolled oats
⅖ cup (100 ml) sunflower seeds
⅖ cup (100 ml) pumpkin seeds
⅖ cup (100 ml) mixed nuts, skinned and coarsely chopped
2 tbsp coconut oil
2 tbsp liquid honey
2 tbsp water
2 tsp acai powder
⅖ cup (100 ml) dried blueberries

Preheat the oven to 302°F (150°C). Line a baking sheet with parchment paper.

Stir together oats, sunflower seeds, pumpkin seeds, and mixed nuts.

Melt the coconut oil over low heat. Mix the coconut oil with the liquid honey and the water. Pour this mix over the oats and seeds on the baking sheet and stir the mixture thoroughly. Dust with the acai powder and stir again.

Place the baking sheet on the lowest rung in the oven, and bake the granola for 35 to 40 minutes. Stir once while baking. Remove the baking sheet from the oven and let the mixture cool completely.

Mix the granola with the dried blueberries. Store the granola in an airtight container at room temperature.

Makes 8 to 10 muffins

OAT AND BLACK CURRANT MUFFINS

You can substitute raspberries or blueberries for black currants. These muffins are very satisfying as breakfast or as a snack with a glass of cold oat milk or a cup of tea. They're also good as a snack with a glass of blood orange juice and coconut water—simply mix equal amounts of blood orange juice and coconut water.

⅘ cup (200 ml) buckwheat flour
⅘ cup (200 ml) rolled oats
2 tbsp potato flour
2 tsp baking powder
¼ tsp (1 krm) salt
2 large eggs
¼ cup (50 ml) liquid honey
1½ banana
⅔ cup (150 ml) oat milk
⅘ cup (200 ml) black currants
2 tbsp black sesame seeds

Preheat the oven to 350°F (175°C). Stir together all dry ingredients in a bowl.

Whisk the eggs and honey in a separate bowl. Peel and blend (or mash) the banana. Whisk it into the egg batter. Add in the oat milk and the dry ingredients. Stir in the black currants and the sesame seeds, saving some seeds for sprinkling on top of the muffins.

Use paper muffins cups inserted into a muffin pan or placed on a flat baking sheet. Divide the batter between the paper cups. Bake the muffins in the middle of the oven for 15 to 20 minutes, or until the muffins are a golden brown.

Serves 6

CORNMEAL CRISPBREAD WITH BEET HUMMUS

The hummus makes a great salad topping, starter, or side dish for lamb and vegetarian dishes.

CORNMEAL CRISPBREAD

⅖ cup (100 ml) sesame seeds
⅔ cup (150 ml) sunflower or pumpkin seeds
⅖ cup (100 ml) corn flour
¼ cup (50 ml) flaxseeds
½ tsp (2 krm) salt
¼ cup (50 ml) cold-pressed canola oil
⅘ cup (200 ml) boiling water
1 tsp sea salt flakes

BEET HUMMUS

3 beets, cooked
2 cloves garlic
1–1¼ cups (200–300 ml) chickpeas, cooked
2 tbsp cold pressed olive oil
⅕–⅖ tsp (1–2 krm) salt
½ tsp (1 krm) freshly ground black pepper

TO SERVE

1 recipe beet hummus (see above)
6 pieces cornmeal crispbread (see above)
3 avocados
Beet sprouts
Pea or sunflower sprouts
Sea salt flakes
Freshly ground black pepper

Preheat the oven to 303°F (150°C). Line a baking sheet with parchment paper.

Mix all the dry ingredients together except for the salt flakes. Stir in the oil and water. Let the dough rest for 15 minutes.

Place the dough on the prepared baking sheet, flatten it slightly with your hand, and place a sheet of parchment paper on top of the dough. With a rolling pin, roll the dough between the sheets of parchment paper until it covers the entire surface of the baking sheet. Remove the top sheet of parchment paper. Sprinkle some salt flakes over the dough, and bake it on the middle rack of the oven for just over 1 hour until the bread is lightly browned around the edges. Let it cool on a cooling rack, and then break it into pieces.

Peel and cut the beets into chunks. Peel and finely chop the garlic. In a food processor mix the beets with the garlic and the chickpeas. Incorporate the oil drop by drop, and season with salt and pepper.

Spread the beet hummus onto the pieces of crisp bread. Halve the avocado and remove the pit. Scoop out the avocado flesh and slice. Place a few slices onto the hummus. Top with beet sprouts and pea or sunflower sprouts. Sprinkle with salt flakes and freshly ground black pepper. Serve the sandwiches immediately.

Serves 4

RED FRUIT SALAD

Spanish chervil, French tarragon, and Thai or Italian basil are other herbs that go very well with this fruit salad. Chervil and tarragon have a slight licorice-like flavor.

ROSEMARY AND HONEY DRESSING
¼ cup (50 ml) honey
¼ cup (50 ml) water
2 sprigs rosemary

RED FRUIT SALAD
¼ watermelon
2 blood oranges
½ quart (½ liter) fresh
  strawberries
1 pomegranate
Rosemary

Mix honey, water, and rosemary in a small saucepan, and warm over medium heat. Let the dressing cool.

Remove the rind and cut up the watermelon into chunks. Peel and slice the oranges. Clean and check the strawberries for grit, then slice or cut them in half. Remove the seeds from the pomegranate.

Place the fruit on a platter and drizzle with the rosemary and honey dressing. Garnish with fresh rosemary.

GLUTEN-FREE SCONES WITH FIG MARMALADE

Scones are always best enjoyed when newly baked, and they're especially tasty when accompanied by fig marmalade and peanut butter (see recipe on page 22). This recipe makes enough for 12 scones and approximately 1 cup of marmalade.

SCONES
1¼ cups (300 ml) soy flour
1⅔ cups (400 ml) rice flour
⅕ cup (50 ml) whole psyllium seeds
⅓ cup (75 ml) psyllium seed husk
2 tsp baking powder
½ tsp (1 krm) salt
5¼ tbsp (75 g) butter
2⅕ cups (500 ml) rice milk
1 tbsp maple syrup

FIG MARMALADE
8 fresh figs
1 bay leaf
2–3 tbsp water
⅖ cup (100 ml) honey or coconut sugar

Preheat the oven to 395°F (200°C). Line a baking sheet with parchment paper.

Mix all the dry ingredients together in a large bowl. Pour the rice milk into a separate bowl.

Melt the butter and pour it into the rice milk. Let the mixture cool down a little. Mix the rice milk and the syrup with the dry ingredients. Mix thoroughly.

Drop dollops of dough onto the prepared baking sheet. Bake them on the middle rack of the oven about 20 to 25 minutes. Let the scones cool on a cooling rack.

Remove the fig stems and chop the fruit into small pieces. Place the fig pieces with the bay leaf and water in a saucepan, and bring to a boil. Keep at a boil for a few minutes, stirring once or twice.

Add the honey or coconut sugar, and let it boil for another 5 minutes or so. Place the marmalade in a jar, put on the lid, and let the marmalade cool.

TIP! The addition of seeds from half a vanilla bean to the figs will make the marmalade even more special. Add them in before boiling the marmalade.

GLUTEN-
FREE
BAKING

Makes 1 loaf of bread

GLUTEN-FREE FRUIT AND NUT BREAD

This bread is wonderful with a cup of tea.

Oil for the baking pan
1¼ oz (35 g) fresh yeast or the equivalent in freeze-dried yeast
2⅓ cups (550 ml) lukewarm water: 98.6°F (37°C)
⅖ cup (100 ml) maple syrup or honey
⅘ cup (200 ml) buckwheat flour
⅘ cup (200 ml) rice flour
⅘ cup (200 ml) corn flour
2 tbsp psyllium husk flour
¼ cup (50 ml) fibrex or NutraFiber Flakes
1 tsp salt
⅘ cup (200 ml) mixture of walnuts and almonds
⅘ cup (200 ml) mixture of dried fruit like figs, raisins and goji berries

Preheat the oven to 355°F (180°C). Grease a round cake pan or a loaf pan with oil, and dust it with buckwheat flour.

Crumble the yeast into a bowl, add the water and syrup, and stir to dissolve the yeast. Stir all dry ingredients together except for the dried fruit, and mix thoroughly. Incorporate the yeasty liquid to make a dough.

Cut off the fig stems and chop the fruit into pieces. Fold fig pieces, raisins, and goji berries into the dough, and leave it to rise, covered with a dishcloth, for about 30 minutes. Transfer the dough to the prepared baking pan and let the dough rise for another 20 minutes or so.

Sprinkle some buckwheat flour over the dough and place the pan on the middle rack of the oven. Bake the bread for about 1 hour. Remove the pan from the oven and let the bread rest in the pan for 5 minutes. Tip the bread onto a cooling rack and let it cool.

Makes 1 loaf of bread

GLUTEN-FREE, FIBER-RICH, RUSTIC BREAD

I like to start my day with this satisfying bread. It's one of my favorites as it reminds me of Danish rye bread. It's loaded with fiber, which is excellent for digestion. Plus, it's wonderful toasted! To switch it up a bit, add ½ cup (100 ml) of goji berries or raisins to the dough.

1¾ oz (50 g) fresh yeast or the equivalent in freeze-dried yeast

3 cups (700 ml) lukewarm water: 98.6°F (37°C)

1¼ cups (300 ml) sunflower seeds

⅖ cup (100 ml) whole flaxseeds

⅖ cup (100 ml) honey

⅔ cup (150 ml) psyllium seeds

2 tsp anise seeds, crushed with mortar and pestle

6¾ oz (200 ml) fibrex or NutraFiber Flakes

1½ tsp salt

1⅔ cups (400 ml) buckwheat flour

⅖ cup (100 ml) buckwheat groats, crushed

⅖ cup (100 ml) psyllium husk flour

Oil for the baking pan

Preheat the oven to 435°F (225°C). Oil a 2-quart loaf pan.

Crumble the yeast into the bowl of a standing mixer, and pour in the water. Add the rest of the ingredients and knead the dough. Let the dough rise in the bowl for about 30 minutes.

Place the dough in the loaf pan and let the dough rise for another 30 minutes.

Sprinkle some buckwheat flour over the dough. Lower the oven temperature to 390°F (200°C), and immediately place the pan on the next-to-lowest rung. Bake for about 1 hour.

Remove the pan from the oven and let the bread rest in the pan for 5 minutes. Tip the bread onto a cooling rack and let it cool under a dishcloth.

TIP! Put sliced avocado onto a piece of bread and sprinkle with sea salt flakes and chili flakes. Incredibly tasty!

VEGAN PLATE WITH SAUERKRAUT AND PUMPKIN PURÉE

So many delectable flavors, all on one plate! I like it when individual foods are kept separate, which allows each ingredient to showcase its own particular taste and color. Taken together, they become a lovely dinner featuring salted nuts, tart red cabbage, and mild pumpkin purée.

RED CABBAGE SAUERKRAUT

1 lb (500 g) (generous) red cabbage
½ tbsp iodine-free salt
1 tbsp caraway seeds

PUMPKIN PURÉE

½ Hokkaido (baby red Hubbard) pumpkin or 1 butternut squash
1 bunch asparagus
3½ oz (100g) mixed nuts (e.g., almonds and cashews)
½ tsp (2 krm) olive oil
⅖ tsp (2 krm) salt
2 avocados
½ red onion

SIDES

14 oz (400 g) cooked black beans
2¾ oz (80 g) mache lettuce
1 tsp white and black sesame seeds
2 tbsp avocado or olive oil
Sea salt flakes
Freshly ground black pepper
1 recipe cashew mayonnaise, see recipe on page 20

Clean and check the red cabbage for grit, then julienne it finely with a slicer or kitchen mandolin. In a bowl, layer salt, cabbage, and caraway seeds. Pound the cabbage with your fist or a mortar so the cabbage wilts and drains its water.

Pack the cabbage as tightly as you can in a glass jar. It's important to eliminate as much oxygen as possible here to make sure the cabbage is completely submerged throughout the pickling process. Set a plate with a heavy weight on top to weigh it down. Let it sit for at least 48 hours at room temperature, around 68–71.6°F (20–22°C).

Place a lid on the jar and let the cabbage rest 10 to 14 days at an ambient temperature of between 59–64.4°F (15–18°C), or store in the refrigerator. It is critical to sterilize the jar if you want to keep the sauerkraut any longer than this. This is done by placing the jar in a 212°F (100°C) oven for 20 minutes.

Peel, remove the seeds, and cut the pumpkin into chunks. Boil the pumpkin in water until soft, approximately 20 minutes. Drain off the water and mash the pumpkin into a puree. Season it with salt and pepper. In a saucepan, bring some lightly salted water to a boil. Boil the asparagus for a few minutes and drain off the water.

Toast the nuts in a dry skillet. Drizzle a few drops of oil over them and season with salt. Leave the nuts to cool on a paper towel. Halve the avocado and remove the pit. Scoop out the avocado flesh. Cut the avocado into segments. Peel and thinly slice the onion.

Arrange lettuce, beans, pumpkin puree, red cabbage, avocado, red onion, and asparagus on plates. Sprinkle nuts and sesame seeds over, and add a dollop of cashew mayonnaise on the side. Finally, scatter avocado or drizzle olive oil over the plate, and sprinkle with sea salt flakes and freshly ground pepper.

TIP! Drink a glass of green juice with this meal for an added boost!

Serves 4

RAW FOOD SALAD WITH BEETS AND CITRONETTE DRESSING

Why not scatter some pumpkin seeds, sunflower seeds, and goji berries over this salad, which gets its slightly sweet-and-sour flavor from the dressing? This salad also makes a great side dish when salmon and chicken are on the menu. For an extra dose of vitamins, serve it with a glass of freshly squeezed orange juice.

SALAD
2 Chioggia beets
1 golden beet
1 carrot
1 bunch radishes
¾ oz (20 g) baby spinach
¾ oz (20 g) pea sprouts
Shiso leaves, daikon greens, or
   garden cress

CITRONETTE DRESSING
1 tsp fresh lemon juice
½–1 tsp liquid honey
2 tbsp cold-pressed canola oil
Pinch of salt
Pinch of freshly ground white
   pepper

Whisk together the ingredients for the citronette dressing.

Peel and thinly slice the Chioggia beets, golden beet, and carrot with a food mandolin, and place on a platter.

Rinse the radishes. Cut them in half if they are large or slice them thinly with the mandolin.

Arrange beets, carrot, radishes, spinach, and pea sprouts on a platter, and snip some garden cress on top.

Drizzle the salad with the dressing.

MELON SALAD WITH CASHEW MAYONNAISE AND ORANGE DRESSING

This is a crisp, sun-yellow, fresh summer salad with a satisfying cashew mayonnaise. Enjoy the salad on its own or as side dish with grilled white meat, such as chicken.

GREEN DISHES

MELON SALAD
3½ oz (100 g) cashew nuts
½ tsp (2 krm) cold-pressed canola or olive oil
1 cantaloupe melon
2¾ oz (80 g) lettuce (mache or arugula work well here)
2½ oz (75 g) alfalfa sprouts
⅖ tsp (2 krm) salt
2 tbsp pumpkin seeds

ORANGE DRESSING
Juice from 1 orange
Grated peel from ½ orange
Juice from 1 lemon
1 tbsp liquid honey
2 tbsp cold-pressed canola oil or olive oil
⅓-inch piece of fresh ginger
Salt
Freshly ground white pepper

CASHEW MAYONNAISE
See recipe on page 20

Mix orange juice, orange peel, and lemon juice for the dressing in a bowl. Whisk in the honey and oil. Peel and grate the ginger, and add it to the dressing. Season with salt and freshly ground white pepper.

Toast the cashews lightly in a dry skillet. Drizzle in the oil and stir a little. Sprinkle with salt, and transfer the nuts to a paper towel.

Peel the melon and remove the seeds. Slice the melon in thin slices and cut them in half in the middle.

Arrange the slices of melon on plates or on a platter. Place lettuce and sprouts on top. Sprinkle nuts and pumpkin seeds over the salad. Drizzle the dressing over and serve with cashew mayonnaise.

Serves 4

"TAKE OUT" SOUPS IN GLASS JARS

Vegetable soup, two ways: one with a base of warm carrot broth and the other with a base of warm Jerusalem artichoke broth. Soups can be so flexible when you brown-bag your lunch.

CARROT BROTH
2 carrots
1¼ cups (300 ml) vegetable stock
½ tsp (2 krm) fresh ginger, grated
¼ fresh red chili pepper or ¼ tsp (2 krm) dried chili flakes
Salt
Freshly ground white pepper

VEGETABLES
1 stalk celery
⅖ cup (100 ml) cooked chickpeas
⅖ cup (100 ml) defrosted edamame beans
⅖ cup (100 ml) cooked black beans
1 tbsp chopped chives
1 tbsp chopped red onion
Basil
Pea sprouts

JERUSALEM ARTICHOKE BROTH
4 Jerusalem artichokes
1 parsnip
1¼ cups (300 ml) vegetable stock
Salt
Freshly ground white pepper

VEGETABLES
2 new potatoes, cooked
¾-inch (2 cm) leek
1 leaf of kale
⅖ cup (100 ml) cooked green peas
⅖ cup (100 ml) cooked kidney beans
Pea sprouts

Juice the carrots. Mix the carrot juice, vegetable stock, and ginger in a saucepan. Chop the chili finely and add to the liquids. Bring to a boil and season with salt and freshly ground white pepper.

Cut the stalk of celery into fine strips. Layer the vegetables in a glass jar. When it's time to eat, bring the carrot broth to a boil and pour it into the jar.

Peel and process the vegetables for the broth in a juice extractor. Mix the juice and vegetable stock in a saucepan. Bring to a boil and season with salt and freshly ground pepper.

Cut the potato into chunks. Julienne the leek and kale. Layer the vegetables in a glass jar. When it's time to eat, heat the Jerusalem artichoke broth and pour it into the jar.

TIP! If you prefer more seasoning in the broths, add in some garlic, ginger, turmeric, and/or chili pepper.

GREEN DISHES

71

SPINACH SALAD WITH GOLDEN BEETS, FIGS, AND GINGER DRESSING

This dish takes its cue from raw food and is perfect for the warmer summer season. During wintertime, I prefer to boil the golden beet pasta for a few minutes in lightly salted water, sauté the spinach with some olive oil and garlic, and serve the dish warm.

GREEN DISHES

SALAD
2 golden beets
½ pomegranate
1¾ oz (50 g) hazelnuts (filberts)
4 figs
1 tbsp honey
3½ oz (100 g) mixed lettuce (e.g., baby spinach and arugula)
1 tsp crushed aniseed

GINGER DRESSING
1 tsp fresh ginger, grated
1 tbsp freshly squeezed lemon juice
1 tsp honey
3 tbsp cold-pressed canola oil

Mix all ingredients for the dressing.

Peel the beets, and put them through a spiral slicer or cut them into very thin strips. Remove the seeds from the pomegranate.

Toast the hazelnuts in a dry skillet. Rub off their skins with a paper towel or a clean dishcloth.

Cut the figs in half down the middle and spread honey over the open, cut sides. With the cut sides down, fry the figs in a warm skillet until the honey has caramelized and is golden brown.

Arrange the salad on a platter. Place the golden beets, figs, and hazelnuts on top, and sprinkle the aniseed on top. Drizzle the dressing over the salad.

Serves 4

ZUCCHINI PASTA WITH BLACK BEAN BALLS AND ARUGULA PESTO

Homemade tomato sauce and zucchini "pappardelle." If you prefer a spicier tomato sauce, try adding in some sliced, fresh red chili pepper.

ARUGULA PESTO
1¾ oz (50 g) arugula
1 container basil
3½ oz (100 g) pine or walnuts
   + ¼ cup (50 ml) extra for garnish
1–2 garlic cloves
¼– ⅔ cup (½–150 ml) cold-pressed olive oil

TOMATO SAUCE
1 yellow onion
2 tomatoes on the vine
½ red bell pepper
2 tbsp olive oil
1¼ cups (300 ml) canned crushed tomatoes
2 garlic cloves
1 tbsp honey
½ tsp (2 krm) salt

BEAN BALLS (makes 20)
14 ⅔ oz (400 g) black beans, cooked
1¼ cups (300 ml) almond flour
1 large egg
1 yellow onion
1 garlic clove
2 tbsp chopped parsley
⅖ tsp (2 krm) freshly ground black pepper
1 tsp salt
Oil for frying

ZUCCHINI PASTA
1 large (or two small) zucchinis
½ tbsp olive oil

Tear the arugula and basil lightly, and chop them in a food processor. Add the nuts, and mix again until they are coarsely chopped. Peel and chop the garlic, and add it to the nut mixture. Add the oil little by little while keeping the food processor running. Toast the extra pine or walnuts lightly in a dry skillet.

Peel and chop the onion, and chop the tomatoes, for the sauce. Remove the seeds and dice the red bell pepper. Sauté the onion in the oil and add in the tomatoes, pepper, and crushed tomatoes. Peel and finely chop the garlic, and mix it with the honey. Simmer the sauce for 8 to 10 minutes; season with salt.

Mash the beans, and stir in the almond flour and egg. Peel and finely grate the onion and garlic, and add them to the bean mixture. Stir in parsley, salt, and pepper. Make the balls and sauté them in the oil until they are nicely browned.

Shave the zucchini in strips lengthwise with a cheese slicer or a kitchen mandolin. Bring some lightly salted water to a boil. Add the zucchini strips to the water and bring back to a boil. Immediately drain off the water and drizzle the cooked zucchini with some oil.

Serve the zucchini pasta with black bean balls, tomato sauce, and arugula pesto. Top it with toasted pine or walnuts.

TIP! This is delicious served with extra arugula and toasted pine or walnuts. Any leftover pesto can be stored in the refrigerator in a jar with a tight-fitting lid. The pesto will keep longer if you add a layer of olive oil on top.

GLUTEN-FREE HAMBURGER BUNS

These are, without a doubt, the tastiest and softest hamburger buns I know. Plus, they are really easy to make. Sprinkle the buns with different seeds and grains for a variety of looks and flavors. Split the buns in half, brush each open side with some oil, and grill or pan-fry them in butter. These buns keep extremely well in the freezer, too. Recipes for three different types of vegetarian burgers follow on the next pages.

BUNS

1½ cups (350 ml) rolled oats
1½ cups (350 ml) rice flour
⅔ cup (150 ml) potato flour or cornstarch
2 tsp salt
½ cup (100 ml) psyllium husk flour
1¾ oz (50 g) fresh yeast or the equivalent in freeze-dried yeast
2 large eggs + 1 large egg for brushing
2 tbsp cold-pressed canola or olive oil
2 tbsp honey
3 cups (700 ml) lukewarm water: 98.6°F (37°C)

GARNISH

For sprinkling on top: 1 tbsp each white and black sesame seeds or ¼ cup (50 ml) pumpkin seeds and 2 tbsp sesame seeds or ¼ cup (50 ml) rolled oats.

Preheat the oven to 390°F (200°C). Line a baking sheet with parchment paper.

Grind the oats in a food processor. Mix all the dry ingredients in a bowl. Crumble the yeast into a separate bowl. Whisk egg, oil, and honey in another bowl. Pour the lukewarm water over the yeast, and add in the egg mixture. Stir in the dry ingredients and mix thoroughly until you have fairly loose and sticky dough. Cover the dough with a kitchen towel, and let it rise for 30 minutes.

Turn the dough out onto a working surface lightly dusted with rice flour; use a dough scraper or rubber spatula to remove the dough from the bowl. Shape the dough into a long rope without kneading out the air.

Divide the dough into 12 pieces. Using a light touch to preserve the air, form round buns, kneading the dough as little as possible.

Set the buns on the prepared baking sheet, cover them with a kitchen towel, and let them rise for another 30 minutes.

Brush the buns with a lightly whisked egg, and sprinkle them with seeds or rolled oats. Bake the buns on the middle rack of the oven for about 20 minutes.

Remove the buns from the oven and let them cool on the baking sheet for a few minutes, then move them to a cooling rack and let them cool under a dish towel.

Serves 8

BEET BURGERS

These are delicious served with either hummus or avocado.

BURGERS
1 white globe onion or 1 yellow onion
1 red onion
2 cloves of garlic
3 cups (700 ml) approx. 1½ lbs (700 g) beets, peeled and grated
⅘ cup (200 ml) rolled oats
⅔ cup (150 ml) buckwheat flour
1½ tbsp cold-pressed canola or olive oil
2 large eggs
½ tsp (2 krm) salt
⅖ tsp (2 krm) freshly ground black pepper
Cold-pressed canola oil or olive oil for frying

Peel and finely mince the onion and garlic. Mix all the ingredients for the burgers together. Shape eight burgers, and fry them on each side over medium heat until they have developed a nice color. Add more salt and pepper if needed.

Peel and slice the red onion.

Split the hamburger buns in two. Grill or fry the cut sides in oil. Arrange lettuce on one half of the bun and top it with the beet burger, avocado, sprouts, and slices of red onion. Place the other half of the bun on top to make the burger.

Serves 8

SWEET POTATO BURGER

Feel free to season the sweet potato burgers with 2 tbsp chopped herbs such as thyme, basil, or parsley. Stir the herbs into the burger mix.

BURGERS
1 yellow onion
2 garlic cloves
3 cups (700 ml) approx. 1½ lbs (700 g) sweet potatoes, peeled and grated
1¼ cups (300 ml) rolled oats
1½ tbsp cold-pressed canola or olive oil
2 large eggs
½ tsp (2 krm) salt
⅖ tsp (2 krm) freshly ground black pepper
2 tbsp chopped basil or parsley
Cold-pressed canola or olive oil for frying

Peel and finely mince the garlic for the mayonnaise. Mix the chili, mayonnaise, and garlic together.

Halve the avocado and remove the pit. Scoop out the avocado flesh and slice into strips lengthwise. Peel and slice the red onion.

Peel and finely mince the onion and garlic for the burgers. Mix all the ingredients together. Shape eight burgers, and fry them on each side over medium heat until they are nicely browned. Add more salt and freshly ground black pepper if needed.

Split the hamburger buns in two. Grill or fry the cut sides in oil.

Arrange lettuce on one half of the bun. Then, add the burger. Top with avocado, sliced red onion, pea sprouts, and red onion slices. Place the other half of the bun on top to form a burger.

MUSHROOM BURGERS

Portabello mushrooms are typically found in well-stocked grocery stores as well as farmers' markets. They taste like wood mushrooms, but are much larger in size.

MUSHROOMS
4 portabello mushrooms
Salt
Freshly ground black pepper
Cold-pressed canola or olive
    oil for frying

Sauté the mushrooms in oil; season them with salt and freshly ground black pepper.

Fry the red onions in oil. Drizzle honey over it toward the end, and let the onions turn golden brown.

Fry some Padrón peppers in a skillet, and season with salt. Split the peppers in half lengthwise.

Peel and finely mince the garlic for the mayonnaise. Mix together the chili, mayonnaise, and garlic.

Slice the buns in half and grill the cut sides or fry them in oil.

Place arugula and lettuce on one half of a bun. Next, add the tomato, mushroom, onion, Padrón peppers, and garlic mayonnaise. Top it all with pea sprouts and place the other half of the bun on top to form a burger.

GREEN DISHES

SIDES TO GO WITH THE BURGERS

SIDES
BEET BURGER

8 burger buns
2 avocados
1 garlic clove
Salt
Freshly ground black pepper
1 red onion
8 lettuce leaves, heart
1 cup (200 ml) (generous)
    beet or alfalfa sprouts

SIDES
SWEET POTATO BURGER

8 burger buns
2 avocados
1 red onion
Mâche lettuce, spinach
1 tomato, sliced
¾ oz (20 g) sunflower sprouts

GARLIC MAYONNAISE
1 clove garlic
1 tbsp chipotle paste or ½ tsp
    (2 krm) chili flakes
4 tbsp mayonnaise or cashew
    mayonnaise
(see recipe page 20)

SIDES
MUSHROOM BURGER

4 burger buns
8 Padrón peppers
¾ oz (20 g) arugula
4 lettuce leaves
1 beef tomato or 2 tomatoes
    on the vine, sliced
34 oz (20 g) pea sprouts

CARAMELIZED RED ONION
1 red onion, sliced
1 tsp liquid honey
salt

GARLIC MAYONNAISE,
    (see recipe on left)

79

Serves 4

ZERO WASTE BURGERS

Save the fiber-rich, wholesome, leftover pulp from juicing vegetables and root vegetables, and turn it into delicious and nutritious burgers.

½ red onion
1 clove garlic
14 oz vegetable pulp (leftover
    from juicing)
1 large egg
1 tbsp cornstarch
½ tsp (2 krm) salt
2 tbsp chopped fresh basil
Cold-pressed canola or olive
    oil for frying
Sea salt flakes
Freshly ground black pepper
    or chili flakes

Peel and finely mince the red onion and garlic clove. Mix all the ingredients together well and form 4 burgers.

Fry the burgers over medium heat a few minutes on each side. Sprinkle with sea salt flakes and pepper.

For example, serve the burgers with sliced tomato, fresh basil, and sliced red onion, or in a hamburger bun (see page 73) with arugula, sliced tomato, sliced red onion, and cashew mayonnaise (see recipe on page 20) spiked with chili and garlic.

Serves 4

SALT-BAKED BEETS WITH LIME-FLAVORED HONEY AND WALNUTS

BEETS
12 small beets
⅔ cup (150 ml) coarse sea salt
2–3 tbsp olive or cold-pressed canola oil
2½ oz (70 g) mixed lettuce leaves
2¼ oz (65 g) walnuts
1 oz (30 g) beet sprouts

LIME-FLAVORED HONEY
1 tbsp honey
Juice of 1 lime
Grated zest of ½ lime
2 tbsp cold-pressed canola or olive oil

Preheat the oven to 390°F (200°C).

Wash the beets and dry them thoroughly. Cut them in half through the middle. Layer a rimmed baking sheet with salt. Place the beets on the salt and drizzle with oil. Bake the beets on the middle rack of the oven for about 20 to 25 minutes or until the beets are soft but still springy to the touch.

Mix together the honey, lime peel, lime juice, and oil.

Toast the walnuts in a dry skillet until they are nicely colored. Chop them coarsely once they've cooled down.

Arrange the lettuce on a platter, place the beets on top, and drizzle with the lime-flavored honey. Sprinkle with the walnuts and beet sprouts.

AVOCADO SOUP WITH SHRIMP

This is by far one of my absolute favorite soups! It's incredibly easy to prepare, and it is deliciously smooth, flavorful, and super satisfying. It contains lots of wholesome ingredients such as good fats, potassium, and minerals that are heart-healthy and essential for good muscle function. Dress the soup up with sprouts and fresh shoots that brim with minerals, vitamins, and enzymes.

Remember to taste the soup before adding any salt. I usually add some herb salt, chopped parsley, or freshly sliced red chili pepper. The soup will be even more substantial and satisfying if you add in whole green peas.

FISH AND SHELLFISH

AVOCADO SOUP

1 quart (1 liter) vegetable stock, made with organic vegetables
4 ripe avocados
Salt
Freshly ground white pepper

TO SERVE

1⅔ cups (400 ml) shrimp, peeled
1½ oz (40 g) pea sprouts
2 tsp white sesame seeds
1 tbsp pumpkin seeds
1 tbsp olive or avocado oil

Bring the vegetable stock to a boil. Halve the avocado and remove the pit. Scoop out the avocado flesh, slice, and place into the stock. Blend the soup with an immersion blender; season with salt and pepper.

Pour the soup into soup plates or bowls. Add the shrimp and pea sprouts, and sprinkle with sesame seeds and pumpkin seeds.

TIP! Avocado oil contains, among other things, beneficial omega-3 and omega-6 vitamins and vitamin E, all of which are excellent for the skin. This also makes avocado oil very good as a bath or shower oil.

Serves 4

GRILLED SQUID WITH FAVA AND CARAMELIZED ONIONS

I spent a few weeks on the Greek island of Santorini these past few summers. I love the sea's deep blue color, the magical quality of the light, and the food prepared from the freshest local produce. The locals regularly serve a dish of grilled squid accompanied with caramelized onions and fava, a side made from lots of creamed garlic and strained yellow peas. This dish is a fantastic dream of flavors. Our version features refreshing arugula and sweet and sour pomegranate seeds.

GRILLED SQUID
8 squid, tubes only
Olive oil
Salt
Freshly ground black pepper

FAVA
1⅔ cups (400 ml) yellow split peas or yellow peas, cooked
2 garlic cloves
2 tbsp warm vegetable stock, made with organic vegetables
2–3 tbsp olive oil
⅖ tsp (2 krm) salt
½ tsp (2 krm) freshly ground black pepper

CARAMELIZED ONIONS
2 yellow onions
1½ tsp honey
Olive oil for frying
Salt
Freshly ground pepper

ACCOMPANIMENT
1½ oz (40 g) arugula
4 lemon wedges
Seeds from 1 pomegranate

Start by finely mincing the garlic for the fava. In a food processor, mix all the ingredients together, and then push the mix through a fine mesh sieve.

Peel and thinly slice the onion. Sauté the onion in the oil over medium heat until it has softened. Drizzle it with the honey and continue to slowly cook until the onion has caramelized to a golden-brown color. Season with salt and pepper.

Clean the squid and remove any cartilage. Rinse the squid and leave it to drain on a clean kitchen towel or a paper towel. Brush the squid with oil and grill on both sides on the grill or in a grill pan on the stove. Season with salt and freshly ground pepper.

Arrange the arugula on plates or on a platter. Add the freshly grilled squid and the lemon wedges, and sprinkle with the pomegranate seeds. Dress with the caramelized onions and serve with the fava.

TIP! I In Greece, fava is typically made with yellow split peas, which are peeled and dried yellow peas. If you can't find split peas, simply strain and use regular yellow peas.

The picture shows a refreshing glass of key lime juice; see recipe on page 28.

TAMARI SALMON, ZUCCHINI SPAGHETTI, ASPARAGUS, AND BROCCOLINI

Feel free to scatter black or white sesame seeds over the salmon.

TAMARI SALMON

1½ lb (600 g) (scant) salmon
  fillet, skin on
Salt
Freshly ground black pepper
2 tbsp olive oil
½ tbsp tamari soy sauce
1 tbsp olive or avocado oil

ZUCCHINI SPAGHETTI

1 zucchini
2 tbsp chopped parsley
2 tbsp chopped basil
1 garlic clove
4 tbsp olive or avocado oil
8 cherry tomatoes
2 tbsp chopped nuts (e.g.,
  cashews)

STEAMED WILD ASPARAGUS

1 bunch green wild asparagus
  or tender green asparagus
1 bamboo leaf or a length of
  kitchen twine, for tying

STEAMED BROCCOLINI

1 bunch broccolini

ACCOMPANIMENT

Sliced limes or lemons

Preheat the oven to 300°F (150°C).

Season the salmon with salt and pepper, and let it sit at room temperature for 10 minutes. Sauté the salmon in oil, skinless side down. Turn the fillet and cook the other side for a few minutes. Place the salmon in the oven and bake it for 10 minutes. Mix the tamari soy sauce and oil, and brush the fish with it.

Put the zucchini through a spiralizer or julienne it into very thin strips. You have the option of serving the zucchini raw or blanched, by quickly dipping it in and out of lightly salted boiling water. Peel and finely mince the garlic. Add it to the herbs, and then add the oil. Stir the strips of zucchini into the herb oil right before serving. Cut the tomatoes in half and add them to the zucchini. Sprinkle with chopped nuts.

Bind the asparagus together. Place them in a bamboo steamer or steam cooker and steam them for 5 to 6 minutes. (If you don't have a steamer, you can bring some water to a boil in a saucepan, put the asparagus in a sieve, balance the sieve in the saucepan above the water, and put a lid on top of the saucepan.) Cook the asparagus for 2 to 3 minutes. Repeat the procedure with the broccolini.

Serve the salmon with the zucchini spaghetti, asparagus, broccolini, and slices of lime or lemon.

TIP! Add diced avocado to the zucchini to make this dish even more delicious. If you can't find broccolini, just use broccoli instead.

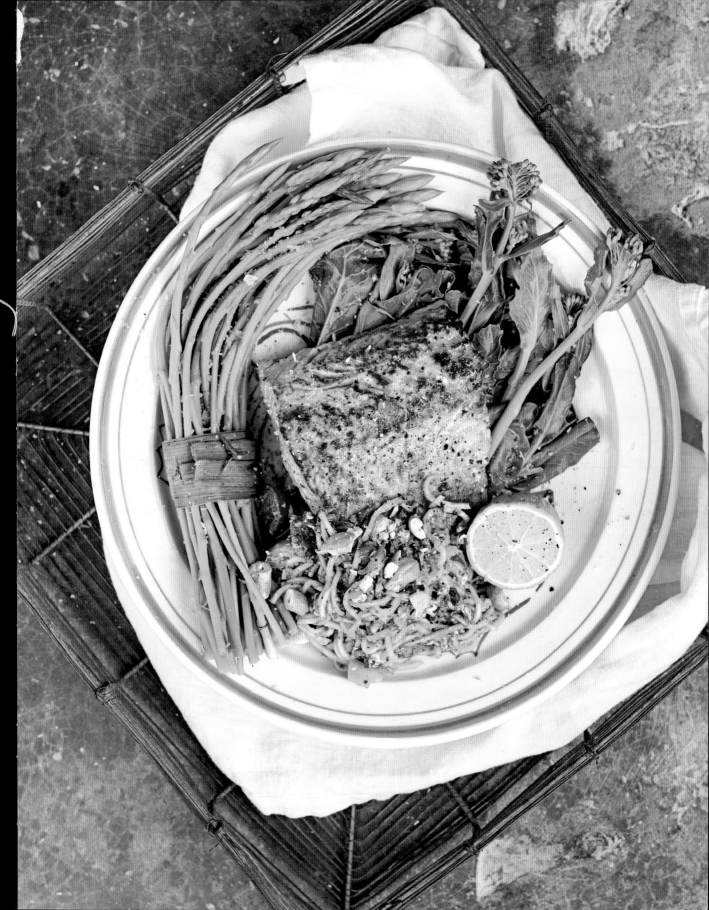

VEGETABLE SPAGHETTI WITH KING CRAB LEGS AND GREEN CURRY

Green curry can be made in many different ways. Add lime leaves if you can find them; they're delicious. You can substitute shrimp for crab claws.

PASTA
2 carrots
1 parsnip
1 zucchini

SHELLFISH
1 lb (500 g/½ kg) (generous) blue mussels
⅘ cup (200 ml) vegetable stock, made with organic vegetables
1 shallot
4 king crab legs, cooked
Cold-pressed canola or olive oil for frying

GREEN CURRY
1 bunch cilantro or Thai basil (reserving some for the garnish)
1–2 garlic cloves
1 lime, juice and grated zest, or 1 stalk lemongrass
½–1 green chili pepper
1 can of coconut milk, approx. 13½ fl oz (400 ml)
Salt
Freshly ground white pepper

Peel the carrots and parsnip for the pasta. Put the carrots, parsnip, and zucchini through a spiralizer.

Peel and finely mince the garlic for the curry. Seed and chop the chili pepper. Process the cilantro or Thai basil, garlic, lime peel, some of the lime juice, and the chili pepper in a mixer to make a green curry paste. Stir the paste into the coconut milk.

Rinse and debeard the mussels, throwing out any open mussels. Bring the stock to a boil. Peel and chop the shallot. Fry the shallot in some oil in a saucepan. Add the mussels to the saucepan, stirring, and add in the hot stock. Place a lid on the saucepan and let the mussels steam until they open—this only takes a few minutes. Remove the saucepan from the heat.

In another saucepan, bring the coconut milk and the curry to a boil; season with salt and pepper.

Bring lightly salted water to a boil in another saucepan and add the spiralized vegetables. Drain immediately.

Arrange the vegetable pasta on plates. Top with mussels, king crab legs, and some sauce. Serve the rest of the sauce in a bowl. Garnish with fresh cilantro.

OVEN-BAKED SEA BASS WITH FRESH COCONUT AND TURMERIC

This is inspired by a dish made by an indigenous people in India, featuring simple, exquisite, and delicious flavors that suit fish so well.

OVEN-BAKED SEA BASS
4 sea bass
Salt
1 coconut
1–3 red chili peppers
1 stalk lemongrass
2 tsp ground turmeric or
    2 whole fresh knobs of
    turmeric
2–3 garlic cloves
2 lime leaves or finely grated
    peel from 1 lime
2 tsp freshly grated ginger
½ tsp sea salt
2–3 garlic cloves

GARNISH
1 bunch cilantro
1 lime

Preheat the oven to 350°F (175°C).

Clean and rinse the fish. Dry with paper towels and place in an ovenproof pan or on a rimmed baking sheet; season with salt and pepper.

Open the coconut and grate the white meat. Place the grated coconut meat in a food processor. Chop one of the chili peppers, the stalk of lemongrass, turmeric, garlic, and lime leaf, and add them to the food processor together with the fresh ginger. Process to a smooth paste, and season with salt.

Spread the coconut paste over the fish. Cut one or two chili peppers lengthwise. Peel the garlic cloves. Place chili and garlic onto the fish, and bake for approximately 25 minutes.

Garnish the fish with cilantro and perhaps a few leaves of lime. Squeeze some lime juice over the fish. Serve immediately, accompanied by a green salad or with some oven-baked sweet potato wedges (see recipe on page 98).

BEET-MARINATED SALMON WITH DIJONNAISE

This makes a perfect appetizer or a light summer meal, and it's really good with a side of asparagus!

BEET-MARINATED SALMON

1 lb (400 g) (scant) salmon fillet, in one piece
2 tbsp salt
4 tbsp coconut sugar
⅖ tsp (2 krm) freshly ground black pepper
1 tsp chili flakes or crumbled mulatto chili
1 beet

DIJONNAISE

3 egg yolks
1½ tbsp apple cider vinegar
2 tbsp coarse-grain Dijon mustard
⅔–1¼ cups (2–300 ml) cold-pressed canola oil
½ tsp (1 krm) salt

GARNISH

1 bunch small beets, cooked
Shiso and daikon cress

Place the salmon, skin-side down, in a pan. Mix salt, coconut sugar, and pepper. Sprinkle the mixture all over the salmon on both top and bottom sides.

Wash the beet thoroughly, peel it with a potato peeler, and rinse it thoroughly again. Coarsely grate the beet and spread it over the salmon. Leave the salmon at room temperature for a couple of hours until the sugar starts to dissolve. Place plastic-wrap over the fish and refrigerate it for 24 hours. Turn the salmon over and leave it for another 24 hours.

Whisk together the egg yolks, vinegar, and mustard. Add the oil in a thin stream while whisking vigorously; season with salt.

Boil the beets in lightly salted water for about 20 minutes. Rub off the skin under cold running water.

Thinly slice the salmon, and arrange the pieces on plates or on a platter. Cut the beets into wedges and place them on the salmon. Sprinkle the cress over the beets. Drizzle with some Dijonnaise, and serve the rest on the side. Fresh beet greens make a lovely garnish.

FISH AND SHELLFISH

GOOD, DELICIOUS & COLORFUL!

95

Serves 4

LOBSTER TACOS

If you like, you can fill the taco shells with salmon instead of lobster. If you do, cut the salmon into approximately 1" x 1" (3 cm x 3 cm) cubes, and fry them in oil. Season with salt and pepper, and serve them with an avocado-and-mango salsa. If someone likes their salsa tangier, just squeeze in some lime juice and add finely grated lime peel.

LOBSTER
2 cooked lobsters

CORNBREAD TORTILLAS
1⅓ cups (400 ml) water
⅔ cup (150 ml) buckwheat flour
⅘ cup (200 ml) corn flour + ⅖ cup (100 ml), for kneading
¼ cup (50 ml) psyllium husk flour
½ tsp (2 krm) salt
½ tbsp honey

AVOCADO-AND-MANGO SALSA
2 avocados
1 mango
½–1 red chili pepper
½ red onion
1 bunch fresh cilantro

ACCOMPANIMENT
Mixed lettuce leaves
2 tbsp mayonnaise
Lime wedges

Cook the lobsters, pick out the meat, and cut the tails in half lengthwise.

Pour the water for the bread into a bowl. Mix all the dry ingredients in a separate bowl. Add the dry ingredients and honey to the water, and mix until you have a dough. Let it sit for 15 minutes. Divide the dough into 12 pieces and form them into round buns. Using a rolling pin on a flat surface dusted with corn flour, roll the buns into 1/16-inch (2 mm) thick rounds. Fry the bread on both sides in a dry skillet.

Halve the avocado and remove the pit. Scoop out the avocado flesh. Dice the avocado and the mango for the salsa. Finely dice the chili. Peel and finely mince the red onion. Chop the cilantro. Mix all the salsa ingredients together.

Place lettuce leaves on the tortillas. Add the lobster meat, a dollop of mayonnaise, and salsa. Serve with lime wedges.

Serves 4

ROAST LAMB WITH CHILI GLAZE, SWEET POTATOES, AND GREEN BEANS

MEAT AND POULTRY

LAMB ROAST
3¼ lb (1½ kg) boneless lamb
   roast
6 garlic cloves
Salt and pepper
2 tbsp olive oil
5 sprigs fresh rosemary

CHILI GLAZE
1 tbsp liquid honey
1 tsp chili flakes
1 tbsp Chinese soy sauce
1 tbsp BBQ sauce
⅖ tsp (2 krm) salt

OVEN-ROASTED SWEET POTATOES
2 sweet potatoes
3 tbsp cold-pressed canola oil
Salt

GREEN BEANS
3½ oz (100 g) green beans

Preheat oven to 350°F (175°C). Trim and neaten the surface of the roast. Season with salt and pepper both inside and out. Peel and chop three of the garlic cloves, and scatter them inside. Add some fresh herbs, and roll up the meat and bind with kitchen twine. Cut small slits into the meat with a sharp knife and insert the rest of the garlic cloves into the cuts. Fry the meat until it is nicely seared all around.

Mix the chili glaze. Place the roast in an oven-proof pan. Drizzle with some olive oil and massage it into the meat. Place the sprigs of rosemary on top of the meat, and bake the roast on the middle rack of the oven for about 1 hour and 20 minutes. The meat is ready when a meat thermometer reads 147–149°F (64–65°C). Baste the roast occasionally with the rendered fat from the roast. Brush the roast with the glaze a few times toward the end of cooking, and once again when the roast is removed from the oven. Cover the roast with a sheet of aluminum foil, and let the roast rest for about 15 minutes before cutting.

Preheat the oven to 435°F (225°C). Wash, dry, and cut the sweet potatoes into wedges. Place them on a rimmed baking sheet lined with parchment paper. Drizzle oil over the wedges, turning them so as to cover them in oil on all sides. Roast the wedges on the middle rack of the oven for about 20 minutes, rotating the wedges halfway through. Remove the baking sheet from the oven and sprinkle the wedges with some salt.

Cook the beans for a few minutes in lightly salted water.

Slice the meat and serve the roast with the sweet potatoes, green beans, and any leftover glaze.

SLOW 'N' LOW BAKED CHICKEN WITH CHIPOTLE GLAZE AND BLACK BEANS

SLOW 'N' LOW CHICKEN
1 free-range chicken
Salt
Freshly ground black pepper
2 tbsp olive or cold-pressed canola oil

CHIPOTLE GLAZE
2 tbsp chipotle paste
2 tbsp olive or cold-pressed canola oil

BLACK BEANS
1 yellow onion
1–2 garlic cloves
14 oz (400 g)/1 can black beans, cooked
2 tbsp olive or cold-pressed canola oil
Salt
Freshly ground black pepper
1 tbsp chopped fresh parsley or cilantro

GRILLED MANGO
1 mango
1 tbsp olive or cold-pressed canola oil

PICO DE GALLO SALSA
3 tomatoes on the vine
1 red or yellow onion
1–2 garlic cloves
1 red chili pepper
½–1 tsp chopped ancho chili
½ yellow, red, or orange bell pepper
½ bunch chopped cilantro, optional
½ tsp (2 krm) salt
1 tbsp olive oil
½–1 lime

Preheat the oven to 302°F (150°C). Season the chicken with salt and pepper, and drizzle it with oil. Place the chicken on a rimmed baking sheet and roast it on the middle rack of the oven for approximately 1½ hours, or until the internal temperature of the chicken reaches 172.4–176°F (78–80°C).

Mix the chipotle paste and oil to make a glaze. When 10 minutes roasting time remains, remove the chicken from the oven and brush it with the glaze. Put the chicken back in the oven to finish cooking; brush the chicken with the glaze again immediately after the roasting is complete.

Peel and finely chop the onion and garlic. Mix the beans with onion and oil. Season with salt and pepper, and fold in the parsley or cilantro.

Peel and cut the mango into wedges. Brush the wedges with oil and grill them in a grill pan or on a grill.

Cut the tomatoes into wedges and remove the seeds. Finely dice the tomato. Peel and finely chop the onion and garlic. Cut the chili into small pieces. Finely dice the bell pepper. Mix everything with the cilantro (if using), oil, salt, and pepper, and finish off by squeezing in some lime juice.

Serve the chicken on a platter together with the beans, Pico de Gallo salsa, and grilled mango.

CARNITAS, GUACAMOLE, AND MANGO SALSA

CARNITAS

1 batch of cornbread tortillas (recipe on page 96)
2¼ lbs (1 kg) pork collar roast, in one piece
½ tsp (2 krm) salt
½ tsp (2 krm) freshly ground white pepper
⅖ tsp (2 krm) ancho chili powder
⅖ tsp (2 krm) paprika powder
1½ tsp coconut sugar
⅖ cup (100 ml) BBQ sauce (see recipe below)
½ quart (500 ml) water
2 tbsp tamari soy sauce
Cold-pressed canola oil or olive oil, for frying

CHILI GLAZE

¼ cup (50 ml) liquid honey
½ tsp (2 krm) chili flakes
1 tbsp tamari soy sauce

BBQ SAUCE

2 tbsp coconut sugar
¼ cup (50 ml) maple syrup
1 tbsp lemon juice, freshly squeezed
4–5 plum tomatoes
¼–½ cup (50–100 ml) water
2 tbsp tamari soy sauce
½ tsp (2 krm) chili flakes

GUACAMOLE

Basic recipe from page 119 (excluding pomegranate seeds)
2 green, yellow, or red tomatoes
½–1 jalapeño pepper
2 tbsp chopped cilantro

MANGO SALSA

1 mango
1 yellow tomato
½ white globe onion
1 tsp lime juice, freshly squeezed

Preheat the oven to 255°F (125°C). Dice the tomatoes, and mix together all the ingredients for the BBQ sauce in a stainless steel saucepan. Cook and reduce for about 10 minutes while stirring. Strain the sauce through a sieve and let it cool.

Rub the pork collar with spices and coconut sugar. Sear the meat on all sides in some oil until it is nicely browned. Place the meat in a lidded, ovenproof pot (a cast-iron Dutch oven, for example) and pour in the BBQ sauce, water, and soy sauce. Put the lid on the pot and place it on the middle rack of the oven. Let it cook for at least 6 to 7 hours. You may need to add some more water during this time. Baste the meat at this time, and turn the meat over at the cooking time's midpoint. The meat will be ready when it is very (fork) tender. Test by using two forks: the meat should easily pull apart. Drain off any remaining liquid and let the meat cool in the pot.

Mix the glaze and brush it onto the meat. Shred the meat.

Finely dice the tomatoes for the guacamole. Peel and finely chop the onion and garlic. Finely chop the jalapeño, too. If you leave in the jalapeño's seeds, the guacamole will be spicier. Halve the avocado and remove the pit. Scoop out the avocado flesh and mash. Mix all the ingredients together.

Peel and dice the mango for the salsa. Dice the tomatoes, and peel and chop the onion. Mix all the ingredients together.

Serve the pulled pork with BBQ sauce, tortillas, guacamole, salsa, and lettuce. Better still, serve some extra avocado and sesame seeds on the side.

Serves 4

TOP SIRLOIN WITH CELLOPHANE NOODLES, TAMARI, AND PEANUTS

If you're a strict adherent to clean food eating, you can substitute zucchini noodles (see recipe on page 75) for the cellophane noodles. The sirloin can be replaced with shrimp, which is especially tasty with a squeeze of lime juice and a drizzle of olive oil.

3½ oz (100 g) cellophane noodles
8 slices top sirloin
½ red onion
2 spring onions, or 4-inch piece of leek
1 red bell pepper
1¾ oz (50 g) arugula
3 tbsp tamari soy sauce
2 tbsp maple syrup
1¾ oz roasted and salted peanuts
½ tsp (2 krm) white and black sesame seeds
1 red chili pepper
8 Padrón peppers
Cilantro for garnish

Boil the cellophane noodles in lightly salted water according to the instructions on the packet.

Peel and julienne the red onion. Finely julienne the spring onions or leek and the bell pepper.

Mix the noodles with the julienned vegetables and arugula.

Mix the soy sauce and maple syrup. Chop the peanuts. Slice the chili pepper. Fry the Padrón peppers in a skillet with some oil.

Arrange the noodles on plates, and serve with top sirloin and Padrón peppers. Serve with the soy sauce and sprinkle with peanuts, sesame seeds, and sliced chili. Garnish with cilantro.

BEEF CHEEKS WITH PURÉE OF JERUSALEM ARTICHOKE AND CASHEWS, WITH PICKLED CHIOGGIA BEETS

BEEF CHEEKS
3 beef cheeks, 14 oz (400 g) each
3 cups (700 ml) meat stock
⅖ cup (100 ml) tamari soy sauce
1 tbsp honey
Salt
⅖ tsp (2 krm) freshly ground white pepper
2 sprigs fresh thyme
1 yellow onion
1 garlic clove
1 carrot
1¾ oz (50 g) celeriac
Oil for frying

JERUSALEM ARTICHOKE AND CASHEW PURÉE
1 cup (250 ml) (heaping) cashew nuts
5–6 Jerusalem artichokes
Juice of 1 lemon
Salt
Freshly ground black pepper

LEMON PICKLED CHIOGGIA BEETS
3 tbsp lemon juice
2 tbsp honey
4 tbsp water
½ tsp mustard seeds
1–2 Chioggia beets

GARNISH
Shiso cress
Pea sprouts
Sesame seeds
Cashew nuts

Start by soaking the cashews for the Jerusalem artichoke purée in water for 5 to 6 hours.

Trim the beef cheeks free of membranes and sinews. Sear the meat in oil; season with salt and pepper. Place the meat in a large pot. Add in stock, soy sauce, honey, and seasoning.

Peel and cut the onion, garlic, and vegetables into small pieces, and brown them in a skillet. Transfer them to the pot with the meat and let simmer for 3 to 4 hours.

Peel the Jerusalem artichokes and place them as you go in a bowl with lemon water to prevent them from discoloring and turning brown. Cut the artichokes in half down the middle and boil them in lightly salted water until they have softened, about 15 to 20 minutes. In a food processor, grind the cashews and add in the artichokes. Process until smooth and season with lemon juice, salt, and pepper.

Whisk together lemon juice, honey, and water for pickling the Chioggia beets. Crush the mustard seeds lightly in a mortar and add to the pickling liquid. Rinse and peel the beets. Slice them thinly with a kitchen mandolin and add them to the pickling liquid.

Cut the beef cheeks down the middle. Serve the meat with the purée and Chioggia beets. Sprinkle Shiso cress, pea sprouts, sesame seeds, and cashew nuts over the dish.

KALE SALAD WITH PICKLED GRAPES, BLUEBERRIES, AND PECANS

This is a truly superb salad found at the farmers' market at the pier in San Francisco, on the American West Coast. There, you'll find many different and wonderful salads in the most tempting and thrilling flavor combos. This salad gets a little extra boost from goji berries.

PICKLED GREEN GRAPES
10½ oz (300 g) green grapes, preferably seedless
⅘ cup (200 ml) water
¼ cup (50 ml) honey
1 lime, juice and grated peel

LIME DRESSING
1 lime, juice and grated peel
1 tsp honey
3 tbsp cold-pressed olive or cold-pressed canola oil

KALE SALAD
4 kale leaves
1 cup (200 ml) blueberries
½ cup (100 ml) goji berries
4 tbsp pumpkin seeds
2¾ oz (75 g) pecans

Rinse and de-stem the grapes. Put the grapes in a glass jar or bowl. Bring water, honey, and lime juice to a boil. Pour the warm liquid over the grapes and stir in the grated lime peel. Place a lid on the jar or bowl and leave the grapes to cool.

Stir together the ingredients for the lime dressing.

Rinse and tear the kale into small pieces, or finely julienne the leaves. Remove the coarse stems.

Arrange the salad on individual plates or in one large bowl. Sprinkle with blueberries, goji berries, pumpkin seeds, and pecan nuts. Top with pickled grapes and pour over the dressing.

Serves 6 to 8

DINOSAUR KALE CHIPS

You can make delightfully crispy chips with dinosaur kale.

1 bunch dinosaur kale
3 tbsp coconut oil
1 tsp sea salt flakes
½ tsp (2 krm) chili flakes
1 tsp dried thyme or
    Mediterranean oregano
1 tsp crushed dried garlic

Preheat the oven to 285°F (140°C). Cut away and remove the thickest part of the kale's stems. Layer kale and coconut oil on a rimmed baking sheet and place the sheet on the middle rack of the oven for 20 to 25 minutes, or until the pieces of kale start drying out. Turn the kale pieces a few times while they're in the oven. Remove the baking sheet from the oven, turn the kale pieces once more, and season with the spices. Let cool.

Serves 4

RAINBOW COLESLAW

I like to sprinkle salads with seeds and nuts as they add both a delicious crunch and great flavor.

2 carrots
½ red onion
7 oz (200 g) green cabbage
7 oz (200 g) red cabbage
½ tart green apple
4 tbsp mayonnaise
Salt
Freshly ground black pepper
1¾ oz (50 g) roasted and
   salted peanuts or cashews,
   coarsely chopped

Peel and finely grate the carrots. Peel the red onion. Thinly shred the green and red cabbage and the onion with a kitchen mandolin. Cut the apple into thin strips.

Mix all the ingredients with the mayonnaise, and season with salt and pepper. Sprinkle with the nuts.

Serves 4

SAN FRANCISCO SALAD

Crisp, crunchy root vegetable salad with avocado, pineapple, and mango is delicious with both fish and chicken. If eaten with fish, add in squeezed lime or lemon juice for extra flavor. If served with chicken, opt for squeezed orange juice and a few fresh slices of red chili pepper.

1 kohlrabi
½ small yellow turnip
   (rutabaga)
¼ pineapple
1 mango
1 avocado
½ zucchini
½ pomegranate
1 tbsp avocado oil or cold-
   pressed olive oil

Peel and cut the kohlrabi and turnip into thin strips. Peel and dice the pineapple into ⅓-inch pieces. Halve the avocado and remove the pit. Scoop out the avocado flesh and cut into pieces. Julienne the zucchini. De-seed the pomegranate.

Mix all the ingredients in a bowl and drizzle with oil.

GREEN GOODIES

Serves 4

RED COLESLAW

You can season the coleslaw with caraways seeds, aniseeds, or fennel seeds according to your personal preference.

14 oz (400 g) red cabbage
2 carrots, regular orange or
    lilac
½ tart green apple
3 spring onions
4–5 tbsp mayonnaise
Salt
Freshly ground black pepper

Shred the red cabbage finely with a kitchen mandolin. Peel the carrots. Finely shred carrots, spring onions, and apple.

Mix all the ingredients (setting aside some spring onion for garnish), and season with salt and pepper. Garnish with some spring onion.

Each recipe serves 4

HUMMUS × 5

Hummus is a chickpea puree from the Middle East. Here are a few of my favorite hummus flavors, inspired by my travels throughout the US.

BASIC HUMMUS

14 oz can (400 g) chickpeas, cooked
2 garlic cloves
1 tbsp tahini (sesame paste)
3 tbsp olive or cold-pressed canola oil
1–2 tsp lemon juice
Salt
Freshly ground black pepper

Drain and rinse the chickpeas under cold water. Peel and chop the garlic.

In a food processor, blend the chickpeas, add in the garlic, and mix again. Add in the tahini and oil, and season with lemon juice, salt, and pepper.

GREEN PEA HUMMUS

2 garlic cloves
1⅔ cups (400 ml) frozen green peas, defrosted
3 sprigs of mint or 2 tbsp chopped chives
2 tbsp olive or cold-pressed canola oil
½ tsp (2 krm) salt
Pinch freshly ground black pepper

Peel and finely chop the garlic. In a food processor, coarsely mix the peas and garlic with the mint or chives. Add in the oil, and season with salt and pepper.

TIP! This hummus goes well with fish, chicken, and vegetarian dishes.

ROASTED BELL PEPPER AND CHILI HUMMUS

1 red bell pepper
14 oz (400 g) can chickpeas, cooked
⅖ tsp (2 krm) chili flakes
1–2 garlic cloves
2 tbsp olive or cold-pressed canola oil
½ tsp (2 krm) salt
Pinch (½ krm) freshly ground black pepper

Preheat the oven to 435°F (225°C). Roast the bell pepper with some oil for 5 to 10 minutes. Let it cool down, and then peel off the skin. Peel and finely chop the garlic.

Drain the chickpeas and rinse them under cold water. In a food processor, blend the chickpeas with the pepper. Add chili flakes and garlic, and mix again. Add in the oil, and season with salt and pepper.

TIP! This hummus goes well with meat, fish, chicken, and salads.

HUMMUS WITH HERBS AND MEDITERRANEAN FLAVORS

14 oz (400 g) can chickpeas, cooked
1–2 garlic cloves
2 tbsp olive or cold-pressed canola oil
½ tbsp tahini (sesame paste)
3 tbsp chopped herbs, basil, rosemary, and chives, for example
1 tsp lemon juice
½ tsp (2 krm) salt
½ tsp (2 krm) freshly ground black pepper

Drain the chickpeas and rinse them under cold water. Peel and finely chop the garlic. In a food processor, mix the chickpeas and garlic. Add in the oil, tahini, herbs, and lemon juice; season with salt and pepper.

TIP! This hummus goes well with lamb, chicken, salad, and Mediterranean dishes.

BLACK BEAN HUMMUS

10½ oz (300 g) can black beans, cooked
3½ (100 g) chickpeas, cooked
2 garlic cloves
2 tbsp olive or cold-pressed canola oil
½ tsp (2 krm) black pepper
⅖ tsp (2 krm) salt
2 tbsp finely chopped red onion

In a food processor, mix the beans with the chickpeas. Peel and finely chop the garlic. Add garlic and oil, and season with salt and pepper. Fold in the red onion.

TIP! This hummus goes well with chicken and vegetarian dishes.

117

Serves 4

GUACAMOLE WITH POMEGRANATE SEEDS

This guacamole is even better if you use the mortar and pestle for mashing the avocado. That way it stays slightly chunky so there's more of a mouthful. If you'd like to spice it up a bit, fold in some finely minced fresh red or green chili peppers. And if you like cilantro, chop up a small bunch and fold it into the mix for the best, freshest flavor yet.

4 ripe avocados
2–3 garlic cloves
Juice of 1 lime
2 tbsp finely chopped yellow
    onion
⅕–⅗ tsp (1–3 krm) salt
½ tsp (2 krm) freshly ground
    black pepper
½ pomegranate

Halve the avocado and remove the pit. Scoop out the avocado flesh. Peel and finely chop the garlic. Using a mortar and pestle or a fork, mash the avocado, together with the lime juice. Mix in the garlic and onion; season with salt and pepper. Remove the seeds from the pomegranate and sprinkle them over the guacamole.

Serves 4

SUGAR SNAP PEAS WITH HONEY AND SALTED CASHEWS

Mange-tout or sugar snap peas are delicious, and they can be enjoyed either cold or warm. In the summertime, I like to have them for a snack or with a drink.

9 oz (250 g) mange-tout or
    sugar snap peas
1 tsp honey
2 tbsp avocado or cold-
    pressed olive oil
2¾ oz (75 g) roasted and
    salted cashews
Sea salt flakes

Put the mange-tout or sugar snap peas in a bowl. Heat the honey and mix it with the oil; drizzle it over the peas. Chop the nuts and scatter them over the peas. Sprinkle with some sea salt flakes.

SERVES 4

DRESSINGS

Dressings are a very simple way to impart more flavor and variety to salads. Here are three of my favorites!

BLACK SESAME SEED DRESSING

1 tbsp black sesame seeds
¼ cup (50 ml) roasted and
   salted peanuts
1 tbsp liquid honey
1 tsp chili flakes
2 tbsp rice vinegar
3 tbsp olive oil
1 tbsp chopped parsley

Whisk all ingredients together.

TIP! This is a wonderfully tasty dressing that goes with just about anything.

TAMARI DRESSING

2 garlic cloves
1 tbsp apple cider vinegar
2 tbsp tamari soy sauce
1 tbsp liquid honey

Peel and finely chop the garlic, and whisk in with the rest of the ingredients.

TIP! This dressing pairs well with warm vegetables, salads, and salmon.

GREEN RAW FOOD DRESSING

1 inch (generous) ginger, fresh
2 jalapeños
1 tbsp agave syrup or liquid
   honey
4 tbsp olive or avocado oil
Juice from ½ lime

Peel and grate the ginger. Cut the stems off the jalapeños. Remove the seeds from the jalapeños for a milder tasting dressing or leave them in for more heat. Whisk all ingredients together for a smooth dressing.

TIP! This dressing goes well with fish, shellfish, salads, and vegetarian dishes.

HOMEGROWN SPROUTS

Sprouts are not only packed with nutrients and vitality, they're also simple and fun to grow at home. They grow quickly, too, when placed directly at the kitchen window. Sprouts are rich in, among other things, trace minerals; vitamins A, B, C, and E; fibers; and life-enhancing enzymes. Sprouts are alkaline and can therefore aid in optimizing the body's pH. Sprouted seeds expand 7 to 8 times in volume, so it's important to select a large enough glass jar to keep them in.

NECESSARY EQUIPMENT

- 1 glass jar
- A piece of cheesecloth to cover jar opening
- 1 rubber band or a length of kitchen twine
- Seeds: China rose radish, lentils (e.g., Beluga lentils), or beans (e.g., mung beans)

DIRECTIONS

Place the seeds, lentils, or beans in the glass jar. Fill the jar with lukewarm water. Let the seeds soak, following the directions in the table below. Pour out the water and place the cloth over the jar's opening, attaching it with the rubber band or kitchen twine. Rinse the sprouts twice daily through the cloth. Place the jar upside down, leaning it on a dish rack for stability, to allow the water to drain out. Leave the sprouts in daylight for 48 hours after they have sprouted to allow them to develop chlorophyll. Continue rinsing the sprouts a few times a day. Store drained sprouts in the refrigerator.

SPROUTING TABLE

SEEDS	AMOUNT	SOAKING TIME	SPROUTING TIME
Alfalfa	3–4 tbsp	5–6 hours	4–5 days
Lentils	1 cup	12 hours	2–3 days
Mung beans	1 cup	12 hours	3–4 days
Chia seeds	3–4 tbsp	7–8 hours	7–9 days
Flax seeds	3–4 tbsp	7–8 hours	7–9 days

THE ICECREAM DREAM

Makes 4 popsicles

CHOCOLATE AND PEANUT ICE CREAM POPSICLES

I love ice cream and wouldn't dream of depriving myself of it! Here is a recipe for wholesome ice pops in two of my favorite flavors: chocolate and peanut.

6 dates
1 banana
⅖ cup (100 ml) coconut milk
1 tbsp almond butter
1 tbsp cocoa
4½ oz (125 g) dark chocolate, 56–64% cacao
¼ cup (50 ml) roasted and salted peanuts, chopped

De-seed the dates. Peel the banana and slice it. Blend all the ingredients in a food processor. Pour the mixture into ice-cream molds and freeze them overnight.

Rinse the bottom of the molds with warm water to loosen the ice pops. Place them on a tray lined with parchment paper and put them back in the freezer.

Melt the chocolate in a stainless steel bowl held over a water bath in a saucepan. Dip the ice pops one by one into the melted chocolate and roll them in the peanuts. Leave the pops in the freezer until you're ready to eat them. Store the ice pops between layers of parchment paper in a plastic, freezer-safe container.

Serves approximately 6

STRAWBERRY RHUBARB ICE CREAM

You can enjoy this ice cream as dessert or as a snack without a guilty conscience. Its texture is slightly different than other ice creams due to its base, which is made of cashew nuts; it is nevertheless refreshing and delicious.

ICE CREAM
8 stalks of rhubarb
⅘ cup (200 ml) raw cashews, soaked in water for 4–6 hours
1 cup (250 ml/250 g) dates, seeds removed
1¼ cups (300 ml) fresh strawberries
½ vanilla bean or ½ tsp (2 krm) vanilla powder
1–2 tbsp liquid honey

MIX-INS
1 pomegranate
1 quart fresh strawberries
1 stalk rhubarb

Rinse and chop the rhubarb into pieces, and process them in a juice extractor.

Drain the water from the cashews and process to a smooth paste. Add in the rhubarb juice. Mix the nuts and the juice. Add in the dates and blend for another minute.

Clean and check the strawberries for grit, and cut them into chunks. Blend them into a smooth puree.

Cut the vanilla bean in half lengthwise and scrape out the seeds—or add the powder or extract—to the ice cream mixture. Sweeten it with honey; if the berries are naturally sweet, 1 tablespoon will be enough.

Store the mixture in the refrigerator for 1 hour, and then churn it in the ice cream machine until creamy. Transfer the ice cream to a container with an airtight lid and store the ice cream in the freezer until it's time to serve.

Cut the pomegranate in half and remove the seeds. Check the strawberries and cut them into chunks. Slice the rhubarb into thin strips with a cheese slicer or potato peeler. Put the strips in ice-cold water and let them sit in the refrigerator for about 30 minutes. Drain the strips right before serving.

Serve the ice cream with pomegranate seeds, strawberries, and rhubarb strips.

ACAI ICE CREAM AND WHEATGRASS ICE CREAM WITH RAWNOLA

Together with Rawnola, these two ice creams become real powerhouses due to all the delicious nutrition packed into one dessert! If you serve the two ice creams together you'll have enough for 4 servings, while each on their own will serve 2.

ACAI ICE CREAM

1 cup (200 ml) frozen
   raspberries
2 bananas, peeled
½–¾ cup (100–150 ml) water
2 tbsp acai powder
½–1 tbsp liquid honey

Peel and slice the bananas. Freeze the bananas for at least 3 hours. In a food processor, mix the bananas and raspberries. Add water, a little at a time, and the acai powder. Sweeten with honey. Store the ice cream in the freezer for 1 hour before serving.

WHEATGRASS ICE CREAM

2 bananas, peeled
1 ripe avocado
2 tbsp wheatgrass powder
½–1 tbsp liquid honey

Peel and slice the bananas and freeze them for at least 3 hours. Halve the avocado and remove the pit. Scoop out the avocado flesh. In a food processor, mix bananas, avocado, and wheatgrass powder. Sweeten with honey. Store the ice cream in the freezer for 1 hour before serving.

TIP! If you'd like to give your ice cream a bit of tang, add in a few drops of lemon juice or some finely grated lemon peel.

RAWNOLA WITH MULBERRIES

⅔ cup (150 ml) rolled oats
8 dates, seeds removed
2 tsp coconut oil
⅔ cup (150 ml) grated
   coconut
⅖ cup (100 ml) dried
   mulberries

In a food processor, mix all the ingredients (except mulberries) together until the mix is grainy. Pour the mixture onto a baking sheet and let it dry at room temperature overnight, or about 12 hours. Stir in the dried mulberries.

TIP! This will make about 8 servings. Save the rest for breakfast or cut the recipe in half.

Serves 4

VEGAN VANILLA ICE CREAM WITH CHOCOLATE SAUCE

This is an egg- and dairy-free vanilla ice cream with two delicious sauces. The recipe makes about one quart (1 liter) of ice cream.

VEGAN VANILLA ICE CREAM

1⅔ cups (400 ml) coconut milk
¼ cup (50 ml) cornstarch
1 vanilla bean
¼ cup (50 ml) neutral-tasting oil (e.g., sunflower, cold-pressed canola, or corn oil)
1¼ cups (300 ml) coconut cream
⅖ cup (100 ml) honey

Whisk together coconut milk and cornstarch in a saucepan. Cut the vanilla bean in half lengthwise and scrape out the seeds. Place both bean and seeds in the saucepan with the coconut milk and cornstarch, and bring to a boil while whisking vigorously. Remove from heat and add in the oil in a thin stream. Whisk in the coconut cream and honey, and place the saucepan in an ice water bath to chill.

Churn the mixture in an ice cream machine; this will take slightly longer than with conventional vanilla ice cream. Serve the ice cream immediately or store it in the freezer. If it is stored in the freezer for longer than 1 hour, you'll have to remove it from the freezer 10 to15 minutes before serving.

Serve the ice cream with chocolate sauce or black carob syrup.

CHOCOLATE SAUCE

½ cup (75 g) coconut oil
¼ cup (50 ml) agave syrup or honey
¼ cup (50 ml) cocoa powder
Pinch of salt
¼ cup (50 ml) coconut cream

Whisk together all ingredients in a saucepan and let them simmer over low heat until the sauce is thoroughly mixed. Serve the sauce lukewarm.

BLACK CAROB SYRUP

¼ cup (50 ml) cocoa powder
½ tsp vanilla powder
Pinch of salt
¼ cup (50 ml) agave syrup or honey
½ tbsp carob powder
¼ cup (50 ml) coconut oil

Whisk together all ingredients in a saucepan, and let the sauce simmer over low heat until it is thoroughly mixed. Serve the sauce lukewarm.

1 pie, approximately 8 servings

BLUEBERRY COCONUT CRUMBLE PIE

Here is a pie that features lots of wonderful flavors: crisp coconut, tasty buckwheat flakes, vanilla, and fat, juicy blueberries.

PIE CRUST
2 cups + 3 tbsp (500 ml) grated coconut
⅔ cup (150 ml) almond flour
⅓ cup (75 ml) coconut oil, softened
2 large eggs
2 tbsp coconut flour
½ tsp (2 krm) vanilla powder

CRUMBLE
⅖ cup (100 ml) buckwheat flakes
¼ cup (50 ml) buckwheat flour
¼ cup (50 ml) grated coconut
¼ cup (50 ml) rolled oats
⅓ cup (75 ml) coconut oil
1½ tbsp honey
2 tsp grated coconut, for sprinkling

FILLING
½ quart (500 ml) blueberries
3 tbsp coconut sugar
1 tbsp cornstarch

LIME-FLAVORED COCONUT CREAM
1¼ cups (300 ml) coconut cream
Finely grated peel of 1 lime
1–2 tsp liquid honey

Preheat the oven to 355°F (180°C). Mix together all the ingredients for the pie crust and make the dough. Place the pastry dough in a pie pan with a diameter of 9½ inches (24 cm) and bake it on the middle rack of the oven for about 10 minutes.

Mix together all the ingredients for crumble, except the last 2 tbsp of coconut reserved for sprinkling. Mix together all the ingredients for the filling. Spread the filling in the prebaked pie crust and cover with the crumble mix. Bake on the middle rack of the oven for about 15 minutes. Sprinkle the reserved grated coconut on top.

Whip up the coconut cream, and add the grated lime peel and the honey.

TIP! If you can't find coconut cream, simply skim off the creamy top layer in a can of coconut milk. The vegan ice cream on page 131 works well with this crumble pie.

Feel free to use other berries, such as raspberries, strawberries, or cherries, instead of blueberries.

Makes 4 individual pies

CRUSTS
⅘ cup (200 ml) almond flour
2–3 tbsp liquid honey
3 tbsp coconut oil
½ tsp (2 krm) ground cinnamon

FILLING
4 tbsp peanut butter
1 tsp lemon juice
1 tbsp liquid honey
1 tart, crisp apple
Ground cinnamon

RAW APPLE TART

Mix all the ingredients for the crust then divide and place in 4 small individual tart pans. Keep the pans in the refrigerator for about 2 hours until the crusts have set.

Divide the peanut butter between the tart pans. Mix the lemon juice and honey. Thinly slice the apple and dip the slices in the lemon-honey mixture. Place the apple slices in the tart crusts and dust with ground cinnamon.

Serves 4 to 6

CHOCOLATE MOUSSE WITH POMEGRANATE AND RASPBERRIES

Make a double batch of chocolate frosting and serve it in small glass jars. Sprinkle the frosting with raspberries, pomegranate seeds, pistachio nuts, and chopped dark chocolate.

Serves approximately 10

SUMMER BERRY TART WITH CASHEW CREAM

Incredibly delectable, and yet so easy to make!

RAW FOOD TART CRUST
1⅔ cups (14 oz/400 g) dates, pitted
⅘ cup (200 ml) cashew nuts
¼–⅖ cup (50–100 ml) coconut oil, softened
¼ cup (50 ml) almond or peanut butter

COCONUT-CASHEW CREAM
⅘ cup (200 ml) raw cashews, soaked for 4 to 6 hours
½ cup (125 ml) almond milk
¼ cup (50 ml) coconut oil, softened
1½ tbsp honey
1 vanilla bean

ACCOMPANIMENT
1 quart (1 liter) assorted berries (e.g., strawberries, black/red currants, blackberries, and/or raspberries)

GARNISH
½ lemon or lime, grated peel

Process the dates and nuts for the crust. Add in coconut oil and almond or peanut butter. Start with one-fourth cup (50 ml) coconut oil and add as needed to get dough that holds together.

Place a round of parchment paper on the bottom of a 7½-inch (19–20 cm) diameter springform pan. Press the mixture into the base of the pan, and place the pan in the refrigerator.

Process the cashews and the almond milk, a little at a time. Add in coconut oil and honey. Cut the vanilla bean in half lengthwise and scrape the vanilla seeds into the filling.

Spread the filling onto the crust and set the pan back in the refrigerator for about 30 minutes.

Slice the strawberries and place them with the other berries onto the tart. Garnish with some grated lemon or lime peel.

VEGAN FUDGE

Store this fudge in the refrigerator and serve it right from there; if you keep it at room temperature the fudge will become too soft. Each fudge recipe makes 15 pieces.

PEANUT BUTTER FUDGE

2–3 tbsp coconut oil
4½ oz (125 g/approx. ½ jar) (scant) peanut butter
2 tbsp coconut cream
2 tbsp liquid honey
½ tsp (2 krm) vanilla powder
2 tsp grated coconut or 1 tsp sea salt flakes

Melt the coconut oil over low heat and add the rest of the ingredients. Stir until it is a smooth mixture. Pour it onto a 4 x 6-inch (10 x 15 cm) rimmed baking pan lined with parchment paper. Set the pan in the freezer until the mixture has firmed up. Sprinkle with grated coconut or some salt flakes, and cut into pieces.

CHOCOLATE FUDGE

1¾ oz (50 g) dark chocolate, 54–65% cacao
2 tbsp coconut oil
1 cup (250 ml) (heaping) peanut or almond butter
¼ cup (50 ml) cocoa powder
1–2 tbsp maple syrup
1 tbsp cacao nibs

Melt the chocolate and coconut oil in separate bowls in the microwave. Mix the peanut butter with the coconut oil. Add in melted chocolate, cacao, and maple syrup. Pour the mixture onto a 4 x 6-inch (10 x 15 cm) rimmed baking pan lined with parchment paper. Set the fudge in the freezer to firm up. Sprinkle with cacao nibs and cut into slices.

LICORICE FUDGE

2–3 tbsp coconut oil
4½ oz (125 g/approx. ½ jar) almond butter
2 tbsp coconut cream
1½ tbsp liquid honey
1 tbsp licorice powder
2 tsp granulated licorice

Melt the coconut oil over low heat, and mix in the rest of the ingredients to make a smooth mixture. Pour the mixture onto a 4 x 6-inch (10 x 15 cm) rimmed baking tray lined with parchment paper. Store the tray in the freezer until the mixture has firmed up. Sprinkle with granulated licorice and cut into pieces.

SWEET & TASTY

Makes about 12 bars

SUPER POWER BARS

I adore these moist bars with crispy chia seeds; they're covered in chocolate and coconut—and taste wonderful. Absolute perfection!

BARS

1 cup (250 ml) walnuts, coarsely chopped
½ cup (100 ml) chia seeds
¼ cup (50 ml) ground flaxseeds
⅓ cup (75 ml) hemp seeds
2 tbsp cacao nibs
⅓ cup (75 ml) grated coconut
⅘ cup (200 ml) pumpkin seeds
⅖ cup (100 ml) dried blueberries or raisins
1 cup (½ lb/250 g) dates, pitted
2–3 tbsp coconut oil

CHOCOLATE SHELL

5¼ oz (150 g) dark chocolate, 54–65% cacao, chopped
1 tbsp coconut oil
2 tbsp grated coconut

In a food processor, mix together all the dry ingredients, setting aside 1¼ cups (300 ml) of the mixture. Mix the remaining ingredients with the dates and coconut oil. Fold in the reserved 1¼ cups (300 ml) of the mix by hand.

Pat the mixture out onto a baking sheet lined with parchment paper, and let the sheet sit in the refrigerator for at least 1 hour.

Melt the chocolate with the coconut oil in the microwave. Pour the chocolate over the bar mixture on the baking sheet and spread it out. Let the chocolate set a little, and then sprinkle it with grated coconut. Cut into bars using a sharp knife.

RAW NUT AND CHOCOLATE BALLS

LIME-FLAVORED PISTACHIO BALLS

These nut and date balls feature a fresh lime flavor. They go really well with a cup of mint tea or a glass of chilled almond milk.

makes about 20 balls

1¼ cups (300 ml) skinless sweet almonds
8 dates, pitted
¼ tsp (1 krm) vanilla powder
Grated peel of 1 lime
Juice of ½ lime
2 tbsp coconut oil
1 tbsp agave syrup or liquid honey
⅔ cup (150 ml) natural pistachio nuts

Grind the almonds coarsely, and add in the dates, vanilla powder, lime peel, lime juice, coconut oil, and agave syrup or honey. Mix until you can shape the mixture into balls.

Chop the pistachios and place them on a plate. Roll the balls in the chopped pistachios. Store the balls in an airtight container in the refrigerator.

CHOCOLATE BALLS WITH CACAO NIBS

Great tasting energy balls with a lot of chocolate flavor. Cacao nibs and chocolate contain, among other things, magnesium and other essential minerals, which will make you feel good.

makes about 24 balls

1¾ oz (50 g) raw or dark chocolate
1¼ cups (300 ml) raw cashew nuts
10 dates, pitted
1 tbsp agave syrup or 1 tbsp liquid honey
1 tbsp raw cacao or regular cocoa powder
⅔ cup (150 ml) cacao nibs

Chop the chocolate in fairly large pieces. Grind the nuts coarsely, and then add in the dates, chocolate, and agave syrup or liquid honey. Mix together all the ingredients and put the mixture in a bowl.

Process the cacao nibs coarsely in a clean bowl in a food processor. Pour them out onto a plate. Roll the nut/chocolate mix into balls and roll them in the cacao nibs.

Store the balls in an airtight container in the refrigerator.

CHOCOLATE BALLS WITH COCONUT

Good to have on hand in the refrigerator when you crave something sweet! These balls freeze very well, too.

makes about 24 balls

1¼ cups (300 ml) raw cashew nuts
10 dates, pitted
¼ cup (50 ml) grated coconut
2 tbsp cocoa powder
2 tbsp coconut oil
½–1 tbsp agave syrup or liquid honey
⅘ cup (200 ml) grated coconut

Grind the cashew nuts coarsely and then add in the dates, ¼-cup grated coconut, cacao, coconut oil, and agave syrup or honey. Mix again until everything is thoroughly mixed and you can roll it into balls.

Pour ⅘-cup grated coconut onto a plate and roll the balls in the coconut.

Store the balls in an airtight container in the refrigerator.

makes about 25 truffles

CHOCOLATE TRUFFLES

These tasty and nutritious vegan truffles require some advance preparation as the nuts need to be soaked overnight. It's up to you to choose which flavor you'd like to infuse them with.

DESSERTS AND RAW SWEETS

7 oz (200 g) raw cashews
5¼ oz (150 g) grated coconut
1¾ oz unhulled sesame seeds
2 tbsp cocoa powder
1 tbsp agave syrup or liquid honey
3½ oz (100 g) dark chocolate (56–70% cacao)
⅔ cup (150 ml) cocoa powder, matcha (green tea powder), or freeze-dried raspberry powder

Soak the cashews in a bowl with cold water. Place a dishtowel over the bowl and leave it at room temperature overnight.

Drain the water and grind the cashews coarsely. Add in the coconut, sesame seeds, cacao, and agave syrup or honey, and mix until you have a paste that can be rolled into balls.

Melt the chocolate in a bowl in the microwave. Roll the truffles first in chocolate and then in cocoa powder to give them a protective and delicious chocolate shell. They keep longer if you follow this step.

Enjoy the truffles immediately. If you prefer to save some in the refrigerator, they will keep better if you roll them in grated coconut.

THANK YOUs

Thank you to my publishing company, Bonnier Fakta, for having faith in me and encouraging me to write the first Swedish edition of this book.

Kerstin Berglund, publisher of the Swedish edition: Many, many thanks, Kerstin, for such great teamwork! I am so grateful to have been given the opportunity to share all these wholesome and delicious recipes. It has been great, Kerstin, to work with you over the years.

Linnéa von Zweigbergk, editor of the Swedish edition: Thank you, Linnéa, for your masterful work. It has been a real pleasure to get to know you over the course of this project. Extra praise for your endless patience!

Elisabeth Björkbom, art director: Thank you, Elisabeth, for all your help. It was great fun to work with you again. Thank you for always being so full of energy and for being so inspiring, and thank you ever so much for bringing the whole team to Mallorca, Spain! It was a wonderful trip during the most beautiful season of the year! And what a joy it was to experience almond and cherry blossoms and huge, ripe citrus fruit all at the same time!

Wolfgang Kleinschmidt, photographer: Thank you, Wolfgang, for your gorgeous and vibrantly colorful pictures. You are so talented! Thank you also for your terrific team spirit and for joining us on Mallorca at such short notice. It was a privilege to work with you, and I hope we can collaborate on many more books in the future!

Thank you, Malin Engblom Namei, for great photo editing/retouch work.

Thanks to Skyhorse Publishing for publishing the English edition of *Clean Cooking* in the United States, and thanks to Kimberley Lim for doing such a good job with the book.

Thank you to the Appelros Aronsen family for letting us become inspired by your wonderful home, *La Fabrica* i *Sóller*, and for allowing us to take this book's photos there, on the island of Mallorca, Spain.

Thank you, Matilda Johansson, my daughter and assistant. It has been so great to have you working with me on this book; you had such a positive influence on all of us. It was wonderful that you were able to be with us on Mallorca. Thank you and thank you, again, for all your help! You are becoming quite the food stylist!

Conny Johansson: As usual, Conny, many thanks for your help!

Kerstin Grabner, my incredible mom! Thank you so much for all your administrative assistance and for everything else you help me with!

Thank you for your inspiration: San Francisco, Los Angeles, Santa Monica, Malibu Farm, Gratitude, Moon Juice, Kreation, and Venice Beach. I am so very happy and grateful that I have been able to visit all these places!

INDEX

Copyright © 2015 by Elisabeth Johansson
First published by Bonnier Fakta, Stockholm, Sweden

English translation © 2016 Skyhorse Publishing

All rights reserved. No part of this book may be reproduced in any manner without the express written consent of the publisher, except in the case of brief excerpts in critical reviews or articles. All inquiries should be addressed to Skyhorse Publishing, 307 West 36th Street, 11th Floor, New York, NY 10018.

Skyhorse Publishing books may be purchased in bulk at special discounts for sales promotion, corporate gifts, fund-raising, or educational purposes. Special editions can also be created to specifications. For details, contact the Special Sales Department, Skyhorse Publishing, 307 West 36th Street, 11th Floor, New York, NY 10018 or info@ skyhorsepublishing.com.

Skyhorse® and Skyhorse Publishing® are registered trademarks of Skyhorse Publishing, Inc.®, a Delaware corporation.

Visit our website at www.skyhorsepublishing.com.

10 9 8 7 6 5 4 3 2 1

Library of Congress Cataloging-in-Publication Data is available on file.

Photos by Wolfgang Kleinschmidt
Design by Elisabeth Björkbom
Cover photo credit by Wolfgang Kleinschmidt

Print ISBN: 978-1-5107-0904-1
Ebook ISBN: 978-1-5107-0907-2

Printed in China